First edition published by Holders Hill Publishing in 2020

Copyright © Nathan Holder, 2020

A Cataloguing-in-Publication catalogue record
for this book is available from the British Library

Paperback ISBN 978 1 9997530 1 6
eBook ISBN 978 1 9997530 2 3

www.thewhybooks.co.uk

Book layout and illustration by Charity Russell
www.charityrussell.com

Why is my PIANO BLACK AND WHITE?

The ultimate fun facts guide

Nathan Holder

Illustrated by Charity Russell

HOLDERS HILL

CONTENTS

INTRODUCTION

This book is all about the piano—obviously! In most cases, when you pick up a piano book, it will tell you where to place your fingers and how to play 'Frère Jacques'. But not this one!

There's so much more to learn about the piano beyond where to find middle C. Join Zaki, Olivia, Callum and Phoebe as they take a look at different genres, pianists, and some of the weirder facts about one of the most popular instruments in the world.

You'll never look at the piano the same way again!

A BRIEF HISTORY

You may have heard of harpsichords, but have you heard of dulcimers, clavichords, virginals and spinets? Probably not! Before the piano was invented, there were other instruments that looked and sounded quite similar. They used different mechanisms and were often much smaller than the pianos we know today. An instrument called the 'harpsichord' was used in Europe as early as the 15th century—some 600 years ago!

Pianos, xylophones, glockenspiels and even triangles are members of the percussion family of instruments. This means that these instruments make sounds when they are hit, shaken or scraped. Some of the earliest instruments that looked like pianos were called 'clavichords' and were invented more than 700 years ago! Later, during the Renaissance and Baroque eras of Western classical music, the harpsichord became the main keyboard instrument. Harpsichord keys were generally made from wood. Often, darker wood would be used for the natural keys, and either ivory or bone was used to decorate the sharps and flats.

Another early form of piano was called the 'fortepiano'.

Fortepiano is a combination of two Italian words — forte and piano — which literally mean 'loud' and 'soft'!

The piano was invented by an Italian named Bartolomeo Cristofori around 1700.

The oldest surviving piano was made by Cristofori himself in 1720. It will have it's 300th birthday in 2020!

For the Cristofori piano, each key usually controlled two strings that were hit, not plucked. This allowed players to have more control over how fast they could play a note, and it gave them more expression.

In the 1730s, in Germany, Gottfried Silbermann invented the sustain pedal and added it to Cristofori's instrument. This pedal allowed notes to still be heard even after a musician stopped pressing on the keys. Try it next time you sit at a piano or keyboard!

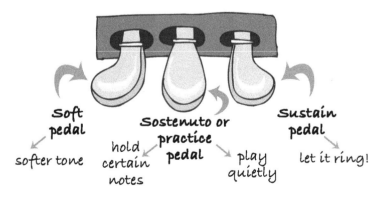

Soft pedal — softer tone

Sostenuto or practice pedal — hold certain notes — play quietly

Sustain pedal — let it ring!

As time went on, the piano evolved in size and shape. Pianos from around the year 1750 only had about five octaves. Yet, by the early 1800s, that was increased to more than seven octaves. Even the amount of strings used for every key increased from two to three.

It is unclear exactly why piano keys changed from the black and white keys of the harpsichord to the ones we all know today. One likely reason is that ivory became very expensive, and in the 1950s it became harder to get. Many piano makers used plastic instead, and in 1989, ivory was banned from piano making in order to help save the elephants who were being killed for it.

These days, there are many different types of pianos:

Concert Grand

The piano you will often see in big concert halls.

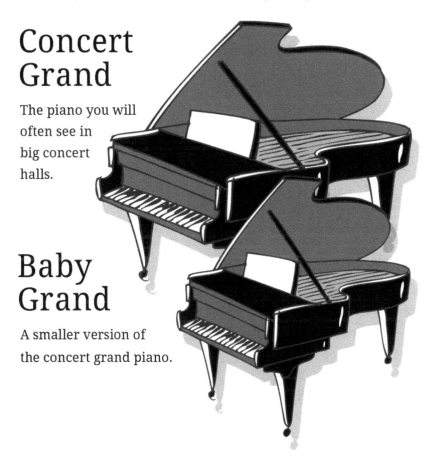

Baby Grand

A smaller version of the concert grand piano.

Toy Piano

Instead of hammers hitting strings inside, they hit metal rods to make a thin and tinny sound.

These pianos are small enough for most people to have at home.

SYNTHESIZER

These come in all shapes and sizes and can produce many different sounds, such as that of violins, trumpets, drums and guitars!

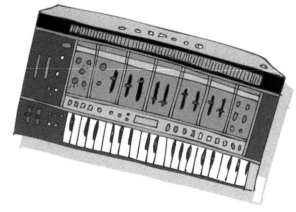

These
pianos
play
themselves!

PLAYER PIANO

These pianos use electricity
(obviously!) to make a
variety of sounds.

Electric
Piano

CLASSICAL

- United States Declaration of Independence (1776)
- Photosynthesis discovered (1779)
- Uranus discovered (1781)
- French Revolution starts (1789)
- Haitian Revolution starts (1791)
- First smallpox vaccination given in Germany (1791)

Haydn was born into a musical family. He began training to play the harpsichord and violin from around age 6. When he was 8, he moved to Vienna where he sang in choirs, learnt music theory and continued playing the harpsichord and violin. In 1757, at 25, Haydn was hired for his first full-time job by the Count Morzin as a Kapellmeister (musical director). He was a good friend of Wolfgang Amadeus Mozart, and they not only performed together but were also fellow Freemasons! He was inspired in the 1770s by a style of music called *Sturm und Drang*, which was an artistic expression of emotional unrest, and his influence spread all over Europe.

Q1:
What does Sturm and Drang mean?
a) Song and Dance
b) Storm and Stress
c) Sand and Dust
d) Melody and Harmony

JOSEPH HAYDN
(1732–1809)
Rohrau, Austria

Haydn also taught many up-and-coming composers, including a young man by the name of Ludwig van Beethoven (more about him later). Haydn's music was eventually being played all over Europe and he moved to the area of Piccadilly Circus in London in 1791.

Haydn composed some of his most famous works in London, including the *Surprise* (1791), *Drumroll* (1795) and *London* (1795) symphonies. He wrote many compositions throughout his life, including 45 piano trios, 62 piano sonatas, 83 string quartets, 14 masses, 26 operas and 107 symphonies. Wow!

In addition to Haydn's outstanding musicianship, historians have written about his great sense of humour and about how generous he was to the people around him.

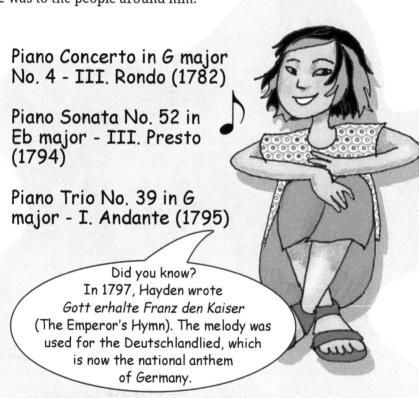

Piano Concerto in G major No. 4 - III. Rondo (1782)

Piano Sonata No. 52 in Eb major - III. Presto (1794)

Piano Trio No. 39 in G major - I. Andante (1795)

Did you know?
In 1797, Hayden wrote
Gott erhalte Franz den Kaiser
(The Emperor's Hymn). The melody was used for the Deutschlandlied, which is now the national anthem of Germany.

230 STRINGS ARE NEEDED FOR A PIANO TO MAKE ITS FULL RANGE OF SOUND!

WOLFGANG AMADEUS MOZART
(1756–91)
Salzburg, Austria

Mozart's father, Leopold, was one of the best music teachers in Austria, so is it surprising that his son became one of the most famous composers ever? When his older sister started to learn the clavichord, the very young Wolfgang showed an interest, so his father decided to teach him. He started composing (with his father's help) when he was only 5 years old! Soon, he became well known across Europe.

Facing many difficulties, the family toured many countries. Mozart, his father and others became sick a few times, and they weren't paid a lot of money, either.

After the tour was over in 1773, Mozart became a court musician in Salzburg where he would first compose piano concertos. Later on that year, Mozart left Salzburg to visit various other cities, including Paris, before settling in Munich in 1781. Joseph Haydn became a big influence on him, and he went on to dedicate six of his quartets to his good friend.

Q2:
How old was Mozart when he wrote his first opera?
a) 11 b) 12 c) 13 d) 14

Fantasia in D minor (1782)

Piano Sonata No. 11 in A major - III. Alla Turca (1783)

Piano Sonata No.16 in C major - I. Allegro (1788)

Q3: Which one of these pets did Mozart have?
a) a dog b) a horse
c) a canary
d) a starling

Salzburg hosts a 'Mozart Week' every year around his birthday, where top performers from all over the world gather for a series of concerts.

WOLFGANG
AMADEUS MOZART

17

Beethoven also showed great musical ability at an early age. And, as with Mozart, Beethoven's father was also a musician and could therefore teach young Ludwig. Beethoven started composing in his early teens and even played the viola in the court orchestra to help support his family after his father died. When he was 21, he went to study with, you guessed it, our friend Joseph Haydn.

Beethoven's reputation as both a composer and a virtuoso pianist grew in Vienna as he continued to write and give public performances. He became one of the first western classical musicians to be paid a salary just to compose. And it was while in Vienna that he wrote his Fifth Symphony, one of the most famous pieces in classical music history.

Unfortunately, in the early 1800s, Beethoven started to lose his hearing, a condition that slowly worsened. But this did not stop him. He continued to compose even after going completely deaf, and when he died, nearly 20,000 people attended his funeral procession. Today, visitors to the Beethoven House in Bonn will see a large collection of special ear horns that he used to improve his hearing.

WOOF!

Q: Did you hear about the vampire who used to torture his victims with his piano playing?
A: His Bach was worse than his bite.

In all, Beethoven composed 722 works including 9 symphonies and 5 piano concertos.

LUDWIG VAN BEETHOVEN
(1770–1827)
Bonn, Germany

Piano Sonata No. 8 in C minor - II. Adagio cantabile (1798)

Piano Sonata No. 14 in C# minor - I. Adagio sostenuto (1801)

Bagatelle No. 25 in A minor (1810)

"Colour is the keyboard, the eyes are the harmonies, the soul is the piano with many strings. The artist is the hand that plays, touching one key or another, to cause vibrations in the soul." – *Wassily Kandinsky*

Q4: 'Bagatelle in A minor' is the real name for which of Beethoven's most famous pieces?

a) Für Elise **b)** The Magic Flute

c) Moonlight Sonata **d)** Symphony No.9

J.C. BACH (1735–82)

J.C. was the youngest son of legendary composer Johann Sebastian Bach. J.C. has often been called 'The English Bach', and during his career he was an influence on such well-known composers as Haydn and Mozart.

FRANCESCA LEBRUN (1756–91)

Lebrun was born in Mannheim, Germany, and was known as a great singer as well as a composer. She came from a very musical family, and her daughters also went on to become well known singers and composers.

ANTON EBERL (1765–1807)

Eberl was a gifted pianist and composer born in Vienna, Austria. He was good friends with Beethoven, and some of his music sounded so similar to Mozart's that it was published by mistake under Mozart's name!

ROMANTIC

- General anaesthetic used for the first time, in Japan (1804)
- Mary Shelly publishes Frankenstein (1818)
- Shaka Zulu dies (1828)
- First electric motor built (1834)
- The country of Liberia founded to help free African-Americans to move out of America (1847)
- The California Gold Rush starts (1848)

As was the case with many famous composers before him, Chopin's parents were also musicians. His father played the flute and violin, and his mother was a piano teacher. From 1823 to 1826, Chopin took organ lessons and gave concerts in Warsaw. He even performed in front of Tsar Alexander I, who gave him a diamond ring. His final report card from the Warsaw Conservatory read, 'exceptional talent, musical genius'.

Chopin started writing the first of his popular études in 1829, and his success as a performer and composer caught the attention of people outside of Warsaw. He left Warsaw for Paris in 1830 and became well respected in western Europe, drawing praise from composers like Robert Schumann, Franz Liszt and Hector Berlioz.

> "Sometimes I can only groan, and suffer, and pour out my despair at the piano."
> - Frederic Chopin

**FRÉDÉRIC CHOPIN
(1810–49)**
Zelazowa Wola, Warsaw,
Poland

Even though he was a masterful pianist, he rarely gave public performances. He concentrated on composing, and his music was published in England, France and Germany. All of his compositions are for the piano, including 21 nocturnes for solo piano.

Over the last seven years of his life, Chopin suffered from many illnesses, and he performed his last public concert on 16th November 1848. He is possibly best known for his nocturnes, mazurkas and sonatas, many of which are technically very difficult.

Nocturne in Eb major No.2 - II. Andante (1830-32)

Piano Sonata No. 2 in Bb minor - III. Funeral (1840)

Nocturne in C# minor (1846)

Deadmau5 used the theme from 'The Funeral March' in his 2008 song 'Ghosts 'n' Stuff'.

When he died, Chopin's heart was removed from his body, preserved and taken to his homeland in Poland.

To: POLAND

Surprise, surprise, Liszt's father was also a musician! The elder Liszt personally knew Haydn and Beethoven. He started teaching Franz when the boy was only 7, and Franz's first piece was published when he was 11, Unfortunately, his father died when he was only 16. Franz soon moved to Paris where he taught the piano. In 1833, he met Chopin and was greatly influenced by him and his music.

Liszt toured Europe and gave many concerts over the next few years. His good looks and incredible skill on the piano turned him into a minor celebrity. In 1842, he was even given an honorary doctorate from the University of Königsberg. But Liszt stopped performing in concerts at age 35 in order to concentrate on composing.

Liszt made a lot of money as a musician, but throughout his life he gave much of it away to various humanitarian causes and charities.

Liszt did, however, stay active on the live music scene by conducting for his close friend and composer Richard Wagner. He moved to Rome in the early 1860s and continued to compose before moving to Budapest and setting up the Royal Academy of Hungary. Some of the most famous people to study there include Eugene Ormandy, Béla Bartók and Zoltán Kodály.

Liszt died in Germany at age 74.

Hungarian Rhapsody No.2 in C# minor (1847)

Liebesträume No.3 (1850)

Grandes études de Paganini in G# minor - La Campanella (1851)

FRANZ LISZT
(1811–86)
Doborján, Hungary

CLARA SCHUMANN
(1819–96)
Leipzig, Germany

Clara's early life was tough. Every day, she had to practise the piano for two hours, as well as undergo lessons in violin, music theory and composition. When she was 9, she met 18-year-old Robert Schumann, whom she would marry 11 years later just before her 21st birthday. Robert went on to become one of the most influential Romantic pianists and composers of all time.

At 18, Clara moved to Vienna, where her reputation grew as a performer. Frédéric Chopin even attended one of her concerts. She was awarded the honour of Royal and Imperial Chamber Virtuoso, which was the highest award given to musicians in Austria at the time.

She travelled, performed and met many musicians, including composer Johannes Brahms and violinist Joseph Joachim, with whom she performed more than 200 times! Clara was also one of the first pianists known for performing pieces from memory.

Her career spanned more than 60 years. In her time, she was well known as a performer, and as a very influential teacher at the Hoch Conservatory in Frankfurt. But it's only been in recent years that people have been performing and recording her compositions, and today she is recognized as one of the most important women in western classical music.

Did you know? Clara used to be featured on the 100 Deutsche Mark bill before Germany switched over to the euro in 2002.

Piano Concerto in A minor - II. Romanza (1836)

Piano Trio in G minor Op. 17 - II. Scherzo (1846)

3 Romances - I. Andante (1853) ♪

While Rachmaninoff started learning the piano when he was 4 years old, he didn't do very well in school. He was sent to the Moscow Conservatory when he was 12 in order to receive a stricter education.

His first—and one of his most well-known—compositions is his *Piano Concerto No.1*, written when he was only 18. He was given a 500-rouble contract to compose, and started to give public performances soon after. His reputation as a performer and composer grew, but when his friend and fellow composer Pytor Ilyich Tchaikovsky died, Rachmaninoff became depressed. He stopped performing for a few years and developed money problems. He eventually made a comeback with his *Piano Concerto No.2*, which, in 1901, earned him the first of his five Glinka Prizes (named in honour of Mikhail Ivanovich Glinka, Russia's first well-known composer).

Rachmaninoff also worked as a conductor and helped to form how the modern orchestra is laid out, including where the conductor stands during performances. He left Russia in 1917, when the Russian Revolution started, and toured Scandinavia before moving permanently to America.

Piano Concerto No.1 F# minor - I. Vivace (1891)

Prelude in C# minor No.2 (1892)

Études-Tableaux Op. 39 in C minor - I. Allegro agitato (1917)

**SERGEI VASILYEVICH
RACHMANINOFF**
(1873–1943)
Semyonovo, Russia

FRANZ SCHUBERT (1797–1828)

Schubert was an early Romantic composer who studied the music of Haydn, Mozart and Beethoven. He wrote more than 600 works before dying at the young age of 31.

FELIX MENDELSSOHN (1809–47)

Born in Hamburg, Germany, Mendelssohn was another early Romantic composer, who wrote the melody for 'Hark! The Herald Angels Sing'. In total he wrote more than 750 works!

ROBERT SCHUMANN (1810–56)

Schumann composed many works for piano and was close friends with composer Johannes Brahms. He died in a mental asylum after trying to take his own life.

JOHANNES BRAHMS (1833-97)

Brahms continued some of the traditions set by Beethoven, Mozart and Haydn. In 1854, he dedicated a piece to his good friend Clara Schumann.

EDWARD ELGAR (1857-1934)

Born in Worchester, England, Elgar was one of the first composers to record using a fancy new technology called the gramophone!

20th CENTURY

- China's Qing Dynasty ends (1912)
- The first FIFA World Cup held, in Uruguay (1930)
- First video game invented (1958)
- Yuri Gagarin of the U.S.S.R. becomes first human in space (1961)
- Indira Gandhi becomes first and only female Prime Minister of India (1966)
- Zimbabwe is the last African country to become independent (1980)

CLAUDE DEBUSSY
(1862–1918)
Paris, France

Debussy was accepted into the Conservertoire de Paris as a pianist when he was only 10. Eventually, he developed a serious interest in composing, winning the Pri de Rome in 1884 for one of his compositions. One of his most popular pieces, *Clair de Lune*, was written in 1890, and it has been featured in many TV shows, movies and even video games.

Debussy's music frequently used the whole tone scale, which can create a very dreamy and slightly sad sound. And he based some of his music on poems, some of which he also wrote. His suite *Pour le piano* (1901), for solo piano, which has been recorded many times, marks a time when Debussy's music took a different direction. He was now using non-traditional harmonies, a style that influenced many composers such as Igor Stravinsky, Pierre Boulez and jazz pianist Bill Evans. Because of the importance of his music, he was made a Chevalier of the Légion d'honneur, the highest award possible for a person in France. Debussy died of colon cancer at age 56.

Q5: Which of these cartoons features 'Clair de Lune'?
a) The Simpsons   b) Phineas and Ferb
c) Dexter's Laboratory
d) SpongeBob SquarePants

2 Arabesques in E major - I. Andantino con moto (1890)

Rêverie (1890)

L'isle joyeuse (1904)

ARNOLD SCHOENBERG
(1874–1951)
Vienna, Austria

Schoenberg pioneered the twelve-tone technique (also known as serialism)—a technique that uses all twelve notes in the chromatic scale. This technique allowed for the music to be played backwards or even upside down, and it makes it very difficult to try and sing any of his melodies!

He was noted as a promising composer early in his life, and much of his music experimented with traditional and new ideas. He lived and worked in Berlin for nine years until Adolf Hitler and the Nazis came to power. Schoenberg was born Jewish, and like many other German-Jewish musicians and scientists, he moved to the United States for safety. In America, he worked as a professor at several universities. He taught many successful composers such as Anton Webern, Alban Berg and John Cage (The Second Viennese School), and he wrote a few books that are still read and studied today. Although Schoenberg's music never really became mainstream, he is still seen as one of the most influential composers of the last 150 years.

Schoenberg was triskaidekaphobic-scared of the number 13!

Drei Klavierstücke Op.11: - I. Massig (1909)

Suite für Klavier Op.25 (1921-1923)

5 Klavierstück Op.23: No.3 - Langsam (1929)

BÉLA VIKTOR JÁNOS BARTÓK
(1881–1945)
Nagyszentmiklós, Hungary

Bartók could play approximately 40 pieces by the time he was 4. And he wrote his first composition, *The Course of the Danube*, when he was only 9!

Bartók studied at the Royal Academy of Music in Budapest and developed an interest in Hungarian folk music. He got a job teaching at the Royal Academy in 1907, and furthered his exploration of Magyar folk music and melodies as he composed *For Children*, a collection of folk tunes for solo piano. He was influenced by Debussy and also studied Bach, Robert Schumann and Johannes Brahms, all the while collecting Hungarian folk melodies.

Bartók had many problems with the government in Hungary, but he continued to compose string quartets, violin sonatas and ballets focused on folk music and peasant melodies. Things gradually worsened, and in 1940, he moved to America to escape World War II, as had many other composers around that time.

Bartók's study of folk music helped to develop ethnomusicology (the study of music in culture and society). Even though he is one of Hungary's greatest classical composers, only 10 people went to his funeral.

Did you know?
There are statues of Bartók in New York City (U.S.A.), Ankara and Târgu Mures (Turkey), Paris (France), London (England), Brussels (Belgium), and Toronto (Canada).

Roman Nepi Tancok (Romanian Folk Dances) (1915)

Mikrokosmos Book 3 No. 70 (1926-1939)

Piano Concerto No.3 BB 127 - I. Allegretto (1945)

Three Dances for Two Prepared Pianos - I. (1945)

34'46.776" For a Pianist (1954)

Swinging (1989)

JOHN CAGE
(1912–92)
Los Angeles, California, U.S.A.

Cage is probably best known for his piece called 4'33. Although there are no notes to play for 4 minutes and 33 seconds, the audience is supposed to pay attention to all the sounds around them—for instance, people coughing or moving in their seats! He was one of the first to introduce the concept of a prepared piano—placing objects like nails, paper and pins between the strings of a piano to alter the sound when the keys were struck.

In the 1930s, he became a student of Arnold Schoenberg in California, who tutored Cage for free after asking him to devote his life to music!

In the 1940s, Cage composed music in a category called "aleatoric (chance)," inventively using a classic Chinese philosophy book, called *I Ching* ("The Book of Changes"). In these compositions, tempo, rhythm, pitch or other musical elements were written by choosing random numbers. For other works, he would write just a few notes, and then instruct performers to play them at any tempo they wanted. He even wrote a piece for an orchestra of 101 musicians!

In 1949, Cage won a National Academy of Arts and Letters award for the invention of the prepared piano.

Queen Elizabeth II owns a piano that was given to Queen Victoria in 1856. The public heard it for the first time on 19th August 2019!

AMY BEACH (1867–1944)
The first American woman to compose and publish a symphony.

ALEXANDER SCRIABIN (1872-1915)
Scriabin influenced many composers of the time including Sergei Prokofiev and Igor Stravinsky. He wrote more than 100 pieces for piano.

MAURICE RAVEL (1875–1937)
One of France's most famous composers, Ravel's music includes elements of jazz and minimalism. He would often write his compositions on the piano, then adapt them for larger ensembles.

SERGEI PROKOFIEV (1891–1953)

Russian composer known for the composition *Peter and the Wolf*, as well as five piano concertos and nine piano sonatas.

KAIKHOSRU SHAPURJI SORABJI (1892–1988)

An English composer who wrote more than 100 works, most of which heavily feature the piano.

DMITRI SHOSTAKOVICH (1906–75)

Russian composer who wrote two piano sonatas and many works for orchestra, including 15 symphonies.

GEORGE WALKER (1922–2018)

In 1996, Walker became the first African American to win a Pulitzer Prize for Music.

EMAHOY TSEGUÉ-MARYAM GUÈBROU (born 1923)

Guèbrou is an Ethiopian nun who has written and performed piano music based on the music of her nation.

21st CENTURY

- The iPod is introduced (2001)
- Facebook begins (2004)
- YouTube was created (2005)
- Rwanda becomes first nation ever to have more women than men in parliament (2008)
- The Burj Khalifa becomes the tallest building in the world (2010)
- Gangnam Style was the first YouTube video to reach 1 billion views (2012)

There are eighty-eight keys on a piano and within that, an entire universe."

— *James Rhodes*

MALEK JANDALI
(born 1972)
Waldbröl, West Germany

Jandali studied music in Syria and America, and his music is heavily influenced by his Syrian heritage. He has performed with many of the world's elite orchestras, including the Royal Philharmonic and the Syrian National Symphony. His 2009 album, *Echoes from Ugarit*, includes his arrangement of the oldest music notation in the world (found in Syria).

Jandali is also well known for his humanitarian work.

'Piano Dream' - Echoes From Ugarit (2009)

'Ya Allah (O God)' (2013)

'An Ocean Without Shores' - Soho (2015)

JAMES RHODES
(born 1975)
London, England, UK

In 2010, Rhodes became the first classical pianist to be signed by a rock label, Warner Bros. His global performances have taken him to Colombia, Barbados and Germany among many other countries. And he has written three books, including *How to Play the Piano* (2016) and *Fire on all Sides* (2018). Rhodes has presented on TV for BBC and Channel 4, and he has been an outspoken campaigner for instrumental teaching in UK schools.

'Widmung' (Dedication), Op.25 No.1 - Jimmy: James Rhodes Live in Brighton (2012)

'Orfeo et Eurydice: Mélodie for Piano Solo' - Five (2014)

Sonata in E minor Op.90: Nicht zu geschwind und sehr singbar vorzutragen - Inside Tracks: The Mixtape (2015)

LANG LANG
(born 1982)
Shenyang, Liaoning, China

Lang started learning the piano when he was only 3 years old and won his first competition at 5! He won many competitions around the world as a child—including events in Germany and Japan—and he moved to the United States at 15 in order to study in Philadelphia.

In 2009, *Time* magazine named him one of the top 100 most influential people on earth, and he has performed for President Barack Obama, Vladimir Putin, Queen Elizabeth II and many other world leaders.

Today, Lang has more than 1 million followers on Instagram, Facebook and Twitter!

'Eight Memories in Watercolour Op.1:1 Missing Moon' - Lang Lang Live at Carnegie Hall (2004)

'Iberia, Book 1: II El Puerto' - Live in Vienna (2010)

Six Pieces for Piano, Volume 2 - 4. La Valse d'Amélie (2019)

Lang was inspired to play the piano after watching the cartoon Tom and Jerry!

KHATIA BUNIATISHVILI
(born 1987)
Batumi, Georgian Soviet Socialist Republic, Soviet Union

Buniatishvili first learnt to play the piano from her mother and quickly became a national superstar. She burst onto the international scene after coming in third in the Arthur Rubinstein International Piano Master Competition, and in 2011, she recorded her first album, titled *Franz Liszt*.

'Mephisto Waltz No.1 S.514' - Liszt: Piano Works (2011)

'Piano Concerto No.3 in D minor Op.30: II - Rachmaninoff: Piano Concertos Nos 2&3 (2017)

Piano Sonata No.21 in Bb major D. 960 - Schubert (2019)

Q: How did the piano get out of jail?
A: With it's keys!

MARTHA ARGERICH (born 1941)

Argerich is an Argentine pianist who released her first commercial recording in 1961. She has won many awards including three Grammys, and a film made about her in 2002 called *Martha Argerich: Evening Conversation*.

CHILLY GONZALES (born 1972)

Gonzales is a pianist and composer from Canada who won a Grammy Award for his work with the electronic duo Daft Punk. He has worked with artists such as Drake, Jarvis Cocker and Puppetmastaz.

YIRUMA (born 1978)

Yiruma was born in South Korea but moved to London when he was 10. He has released many albums and performed around the world, including in Singapore, Australia, Russia and the United States.

YUJA WANG (born 1987)

Wang has performed with some of the top orchestras in the world, including the Berlin Philharmonic and the Hong Kong Philharmonic. Her performance of Rimsky-Korsakov's 'Flight of the Bumblebee' in 2011 has nearly 11 million views on various YouTube videos!

RAGTIME
SCOTT JOPLIN
(1868–1917)
Texarkana, Arkansas, U.S.A.

Joplin was born into a musical family and started playing the piano when he was about 7. He received free lessons from a music professor, who taught him about classical and opera music. He also sang in a vocal quartet and taught the mandolin and guitar.

Joplin traveled and performed even though there weren't too many opportunities for black piano players at the time. He became well known at a few clubs in Missouri and had two of his compositions published in 1895. One of his most famous pieces, 'Maple Leaf Rag', was published in 1899 and became one of the most influential ragtime pieces ever.

Joplin also wrote an opera called Treemonisha, but unfortunately it didn't do very well. It was performed in full in 1972, however, and Joplin was awarded the Pulitzer Prize even though he had died many years before. He never made any recordings, but he created seven piano rolls, so his playing is preserved. He is now commonly known as the King of Ragtime.

Did you know?
Scott Joplin has a star on the St Louis Walk of Fame.

Work as a pianist was difficult as black performers in the 1890s were discriminated against. For much of their lives, many of the composers and performers in early jazz history had to deal with racism.

'The Entertainer' (1902)

'Weeping Willow' (1903)

'Magnetic Rag' (1914)

The most expensive piano is called the Crystal Piano which was sold for $3.22 million!! The first person to play publicly on the Crystal Piano was pianist Lang Lang who performed at the Beijing Olympics in 2008.

JELLY ROLL MORTON
(1890–1941)
New Orleans, Louisiana, U.S.A.

Jelly Roll (real name, Ferdinand LaMothe) started to play around town when he was only 14, and he quickly became well known. His grandmother was very religious and kicked him out of the house for playing jazz, which she called 'devil music'. He toured across America performing in minstrel shows and composing his own music. Some of his most famous compositions, like 'King Porter Stomp', were composed around 1904 but were published years later.

His tune 'Jelly Roll Blues' was arguably the first-ever-published jazz composition. 'King Porter Stomp' became a big hit for clarinetist Benny Goodman, but Jelly Roll received no money from its success. As his music eventually went out of fashion, he found it difficult to get enough work.

In 1938, Jelly Roll recorded music and gave interviews for the Library of Congress, which helped to preserve his importance in early jazz history. He recorded with many famous musicians of the time, such as clarinetists Artie Shaw and Sidney Bechet, and was inducted into the Louisiana Music Hall of Fame in 2008.

'Kansas City Stomp' (1923)

'Wolverine Blues' (1923)

'Black Bottom Stomp' (1925)

"A pianist is a painter of music"
— Goitsemang Mvula

JAMES P. JOHNSON
(1894–1955)
New Jersey, U.S.A.

Johnson grew up listening to Scott Joplin's music, and because he had perfect pitch, it didn't take him long to learn many of the tunes he heard. He decided to pursue a career in music at 16, and began by studying pianists from Europe as well as ragtime music. He was one of the most important Harlem stride piano players and was pivotal in evolving ragtime into early jazz.

Johnson recorded a few of his compositions 1921, which were among the first few jazz piano solos to be released. He went on to compose for musical theatre, and he also created the popular work, *Yamekraw – A Negro Rhapsody* (1927). Among the many musicians he performed with are trumpeter Louis Armstrong, clarinetist Sidney Bechet and singer Bessie Smith. Thomas 'Fats' Waller was one of his most famous students, and he directly influenced pianists Duke Ellington, Count Basie and Louis Mazetier. He was inducted into the *DownBeat* (a popular jazz magazine) Jazz Hall of Fame in 1973.

Did you know?
In 1995, the U.S. Postal Service created a 32¢ stamp in memory of James Johnson.

Polish musician Romuald Koperski holds the record for the longest piano concert ever held: 103 hours and 8 seconds long. Thats over 4 days!

Q: Why are pianos so hard to open?

A: The keys are inside!

JAMES SCOTT (1885–1938)

Even though Scott's parents were born slaves, he published more than 35 rags for piano and is considered as one of the most important ragtime composers.

EUBIE BLAKE (1887–1983)

Born in Baltimore, Blake wrote many tunes for musicals and was one of the first African Americans to write and direct a Broadway musical. He was given the Presidential Medal of Freedom in 1981.

JOSEPH LAMB (1887–1960)

Another important ragtime composer. Lamb often used long phrases influenced by classical music in his pieces such as 'Ethiopia Rag' (1909) and 'The Ragtime Nightingale' (1915). He only made one recording in his lifetime.

SWING

EDWARD 'DUKE' ELLINGTON
(1899–1974)
Washington, D.C., U.S.A.

In a career that spanned 60 years, Ellington composed more than 1000 tunes and performed with many of jazz's greatest musicians. He was given the name 'Duke' because of his elegant style and dress sense. He grew up in Washington D.C, and once saw the President of the United States ride past his local baseball field on a horse! As a boy, he developed a gradual interest in the piano, learnt to read music and was inspired by our friends James P. Johnson, Fats Waller and Debussy.

In 1927, he became the leader of an eleven-piece orchestra at Harlem's Cotton Club. Word soon got around about his impressive talent. He was soon working in movies and recording what would become jazz standards like 'It Don't Mean A Thing (If It Ain't Got That Swing)' (1932) and 'In A Sentimental Mood' (1935).

Ellington won 14 Grammy Awards including Best Original Jazz Composition (1964, 1965, 1966), Best Instrumental Composition (1971) and Best Jazz Performance By A Big Band (1971, 1972, 1976). He recorded with many famous artists, including singers Ella Fitzgerald and Frank Sinatra, saxophonist John Coltrane and Louis Armstrong. Many tunes have been written in his honour, including 'Sir Duke' (1976) by Stevie Wonder.

Duke Ellington was awarded the Presidential Medal of Freedom in 1969 by U.S. President Richard Nixon.

'Sophisticated Lady' (1932)

'Caravan' (1936)

'Satin Doll' (1953)

ART TATUM JR
(1909–56)
Toledo, Ohio, U.S.A.

Art Tatum learnt how to play the piano by teaching himself tunes from the radio and by being involved in the music in his local church. While he was still a teenager, bandleaders Fletcher Henderson and Duke Ellington heard him play and were impressed with his technique and ability. Soon after, he moved to New York to play with a singer called Adelaide Hall, with whom he recorded his first tunes.

Legend has it that Tatum 'battled' James P. Johnson and Fats Waller on the piano in New York and soon established himself there as one of the top jazz pianists. He continued to record and play in clubs in New York, Cleveland and Chicago, even travelling to England for a few months in 1938. Unfortunately, he developed a bad drinking habit during this time. Many musicians today talk about his incredible speed, touch and how he used harmony in ways that no one else had before.

Tatum won the *DownBeat* Best Pianist award three years in a row and recorded and performed across America up until a month before his death in 1956. His version of the song 'Tea for Two', which he recorded in 1939, won a Grammy Hall of Fame Award in 1986.

Art Tatum was blind in one eye and partially sighted in the other.

'Sweet Lorraine' - Piano Solos (1940)

'Tea for Two' - Piano Solos Vol. 2 (1950)

'Come Rain Or Come Shine' - The
Genius of Art Tatum (1954)

MARY LOU WILLIAMS
(1910-81)
Pittsburgh, Pennsylvania, U.S.A.

Williams taught herself to play the piano at age 3 and was known in her hometown as 'The Little Piano Girl'. She moved to Kansas City, Missouri, in 1929 and started arranging and recording with bands and as a solo artist. As her reputation grew, she worked with a range of musicians, including pianist Earl Hines, Benny Goodman, trumpeter Dizzy Gillespie and drummer Art Blakey. She also composed *Zodiac Suite* (1945), a 40-minute classically influenced composition in 12 parts (one for each sign of the zodiac).

Williams became a Roman Catholic in 1956 and composed jazz music focused on her new faith with tunes like 'Black Christ of the Andes' (1963) and 'Mary Lou's Mass' (1975). The 1970s were perhaps her most successful decade as she recorded many albums, performed at various jazz festivals and became the artist-in-residence at Duke University.

She died in 1981 and has been recognized as one of the most important women in jazz history. Duke University founded the Mary Lou Williams Center for Black Culture in 1983, and The Mary Lou Williams Women in Jazz Festival was established in 1996 and is held annually in her honour in Washington, D.C.

'A Fungus Amungus' - Mary Lou Williams (1964)

'Praise the Lord' - Zoning (1974)

'Roll 'Em' - Live At The Cookery (1976)

NAT KING COLE
(1919-65)
Montgomery, Alabama, U.S.A.

Cole heard Earl Hines and Louis Armstrong play as a teenager, and began playing professionally in Los Angeles in the late 1930s. Some of his most famous hits include '(I Love You) For Sentimental Reasons' (1946) and 'Too Young' (1950). He was the first African American man to host a TV series and performed and recorded with musicians such as Lester Young, percussionist Jack Costanzo and arranger Ralph Carmichael. He won a Grammy Lifetime Acheivement Award in 1990 and has four songs in the Grammy Hall of Fame.

Did you know? When Nat King Cole died, his honorary pall bearers included Sammy Davis Jr, Frank Sinatra and Count Basie.

'Straighten Up and Fly Right' (1943)

'(I Love You) For Sentimental Reasons' - The Nat King Cole Story (1961)

'The Christmas Song' - The Nat King Cole Story (1961)

EARL HINES (1903–83)

Hines played with Louis Armstrong, Ella Fitzgerald and saxophonist Charlie Parker. He was known for his use of syncopation and improvising with tremolos, which many people said made him sound as if he was playing a trumpet. Hines performed twice at the White House and also for Pope Paul IV.

THOMAS 'FATS' WALLER (1904–43)

Waller wrote jazz standards such as 'Ain't Misbehavin' (1929) and 'Honeysuckle Rose' (1929). His stride piano style helped to influence other pianists, such as Count Basie and Erroll Garner.

TEDDY WILSON (1912–86)

An important member of the Benny Goodman Trio and Quartet at a time when black and white musicians rarely performed together. Wilson also performed with saxophonists Lester Young and Ben Webster, vocalist Sarah Vaughn, and other jazz greats. He worked as a music director for U.S. television talk show, The Dick Cavett Show.

"I'm an interpreter of stories. When I perform it's like sitting down at my piano and telling fairy stories."
-Nat King Cole

BEBOP

THELONIOUS MONK
(1917–82)
Rocky Mount, North Carolina, U.S.A.

Monk began learning the piano at about 6 years old, and by 17, he was playing the church organ while exploring jazz. He became the house pianist in a New York nightclub called Minton's Playhouse, which would become one of the most important places for the evolution of bebop.

As a teenager, Monk knew James P Johnson, and he was spotted by Mary Lou Williams while he was playing at Minton's. He performed and recorded with many of the major jazz musicians of his time including saxophonist Sonny Rollins, drummer Roy Haynes and trumpeter Miles Davis. A very interesting performer to watch, he would dress differently from most other musicians, and he would sometimes get up from the piano to dance and clap.

Many of Monk's compositions are quite difficult, like 'Epistrophy' (1941) and 'Introspection' (1944). He used a lot of space in his solos and would often hit two or three keys at the same time. By the time he died, he was the second-most-recorded jazz composer of all time. In 1993, he was awarded a Grammy Lifetime Achievement Award, and a Pulitzer Prize in 2006.

Did you know? Many of his pieces were written in the key of Bb.

'Round Midnight' (1944)

'Well, You Needn't' - Genius Of Modern Music Vol.1 (1947)

'Blue Monk' - Thelonious Monk Trio (1954)

HANK JONES
(1918–2010)
Vicksburg, Mississippi, U.S.A.

How many people can say that they have recorded more than 60 albums? Hank Jones is one of them! He came from one of the most musical families in jazz history, with his younger brothers Thad Jones (Trumpet) and Elvin Jones (Drums) becoming important jazz musicians themselves.

Jones was performing regularly by the time he was 13, and soon after, he moved to New York to play with saxophonist Lucky Thompson. He went on to play with vocalist Ella Fitzgerald for five years and performed with clarinetists Benny Goodman, Artie Shaw and vocalist Frank Sinatra. He also worked as a pianist and conductor for the musical *Ain't Misbehavin'* (based on the music of Fats Waller).

Jones performed on iconic albums like saxophonist Cannonball Adderley's *Somethin' Else* (1958) and even on an Afro-pop record with a West African ensemble from Mali called *Steel Away* (1995). He had a long, productive life. At 91, he performed in Japan, and he appeared in a documentary about the making of a Steinway Piano in 2007. He was nominated for five Grammy Awards, given an honorary doctorate from Berklee College of Music in 2005, and received the National Medal of Arts in 2008.

'Summertime' - Porgy and Bess (1959)

'I'll Remember April' - The Trio (1977) ♪

'Eleanor' - West Of 5th (2006)

Did you know?
Hank Jones played the piano when
Marilyn Monroe sang 'Happy Birthday'
to John. F. Kennedy!

'Bouncing with Bud' (1946)

'Un Poco Loco' - The Amazing Bud Powell Vol.1 (1951)

'Glass Enclosure' - The Amazing Bud Powell Vol.2 (1953)

Q8: In 'Walked Bud' (1947) is a tune dedicated to Bud Powell, but who wrote it?
a) Thelonius Monk **b)** Nat King Cole
c) Duke Ellington **d)** Oscar Peterson

BUD POWELL
(1924–66)
New York City (Harlem), New York, U.S.A.

Powell started learning classical music as a young boy but within a few years became interested in swing music. Like so many others, he also came from a musical family — his father and older brother were also musicians.

The first piece Powell could play really well was James P. Johnson's 'Carolina Shout' (1921), and soon after, he was mentored by Thelonious Monk. In addition, he was heavily influenced by Art Tatum and Fats Waller, and he also heard Charlie Parker play live at a young age. As Powell's experience and reputation grew, Parker invited him to record with him, Miles Davis and drummer Max Roach. Powell's style of improvising was very similar to how saxophone and trumpet players played, and he helped to expand the possibilities open to piano players.

Powell recorded and performed with musicians like Art Blakey and trumpeters Fats Navarro and Cootie Williams. Unfortunately, he battled health problems for much of his life, and he was sent to mental hospitals for months at a time. Even through all of this, he recorded, performed and toured with many musicians until a decline in his mental health stopped him from performing at a high level.

Powell inspired several famous pianists, such as McCoy Tyner, Chick Corea and Herbie Hancock.

"The piano ain't got no wrong notes."
- Thelonious Monk

OSCAR PETERSON (1925–2007)

In his long career, Peterson won eight Grammy Awards and worked with musicians like Dizzy Gillespie, Ella Fitzgerald and guitarist Joe Pass. He was also known for incorporating well known melodies — including some by Sergei Rachmaninoff — in his solos.

BARRY HARRIS (born 1929)

Harris was influenced by Thelonious Monk and Bud Powell. He has performed with saxophonists Cannonball Adderley, Coleman Hawkins, and with Miles Davis to name a few. He has many jazz theory videos on YouTube and was awarded the Special Presidential Award Recognition of Dedication and Commitment to the Pursuance of Artistic Excellence in Jazz Performance and Education in 1995.

WYNTON KELLY (1931–71)

Kelly was an important, blues-influenced pianist, who played with many jazz greats including saxophonists John Coltrane, Hank Mobley and Rahsaan Roland Kirk; guitarist Wes Montgomery and vocalist Billie Holiday. He played on the classic Miles Davis album *Kind Of Blue* (1959) before setting up his own trio with bassist Jimmy Cobb and drummer Paul Chambers. His influence was so big that trumpeter Wynton Marsalis was named after him!

"What has keys but
can't listen to the beauty
it unlocks? A piano."

– *Jarod Kintz*

COOL

MARIAN MCPARTLAND
(1918–2013)
Slough, UK

Marian McPartland didn't have a traditional musical education as a young girl, but since she had perfect pitch, she learned mostly by listening to records and then playing what she heard. She studied at London's Guildhall School of Music and Drama and, while there, won prizes for improvising and composition. She avoided being drafted into the army by joining the United Service Organizations (USO) in 1944 and performing for the American soldiers. She met and married her husband while in Europe and after the war, moved to the United States to perform and compose. She performed with musicians such as vocalist Billie Holiday, saxophonist Coleman Hawkins and trumpeter Roy Eldridge.

In the 1950s, McPartland wrote for various magazines about what it was like to be a woman in jazz. She founded her own record label — Halcyon Records — in 1969, and went on to headline the first-ever Women's Jazz Festival in Kansas City in 1978. In 1979, the *Marian McPartland Piano Jazz* program began on NPR, and it ran for 25 years! Her list of awards and honours is very impressive, including a Mary Lou Williams Women in Jazz Award in 2000, being inducted into the National Radio Hall of Fame in 2007, and earning an OBE in 2010.

Q9: Who was Marian McPartland's first guest on her radio show?
   a) Duke Ellington **b)** Dave Brubeck
   c) Mary Lou Williams **d)** George Duke

'In Your Own Sweet Way' - Brubeck Plays Brubeck (1956)

'Blue Rondo à La Turk' - Time Out (1959)

'Unsquare Dance' (1961)

DAVE BRUBECK
(1920–2012)
Concord, California, U.S.A.

Dave Brubeck was well known for experimenting with different time signatures, such as 9/8, 7/4 and 13/4. Like his time signatures, the start of his music career was also non-traditional. In fact, he had originally wanted to become a veterinarian! Brubeck was drafted into the army in 1942, and there he started one of its first racially mixed bands (before then, black people and white people weren't allowed to perform together). While in the army, he had a couple of lessons with Arnold Schoenberg, which influenced some of his later music.

In 1951, Brubeck had a bad accident in Hawaii, which forced him to develop a playing style that involved playing more chords than fast runs when he took solos. That year, he teamed up with saxophonist Paul Desmond to form the Dave Brubeck Quartet, and they recorded some of his most famous work together. In 1959, his most famous album, *Time Out*, was released, which became the first jazz album to sell more than one million copies!

The Dave Brubeck Quartet continued to record and perform under slightly different names and with various band members — one formation was even made up of Brubeck and his sons Chris, Darius and Dan! — until his death in 2012. He won a Grammy Lifetime Acheivement Award in 1996 and received multiple honorary degrees and awards.

> "It's like a whole orchestra, the piano for me."
> -Dave Brubeck

BILL EVANS
(1929–80)
Plainfield, New Jersey, U.S.A.

Bill Evans is another pianist who started playing classical music as a child. He took lessons seriously, and unlike many other jazz pianists, he went to college and earned Bachelor of Music and Bachelor of Music Education degrees. He was heavily influenced by classical composers such as Debussy and Bach. Even though he became known as a pianist, he also learned the violin, flute and piccolo and played flute and piccolo while in the army from 1951 to 1954. During that time he wrote one of his most famous pieces, 'Waltz for Debby'.

After the army, Evans moved back to New York where he met musicians like Miles Davis and Thelonious Monk. He recorded his first album, *New Jazz Conceptions*, in 1956. It received good reviews but didn't sell very well at first. A few years later, after working on and off with Miles Davis, Evans played on and helped to compose some music on the best-selling jazz album of all time, *Kind Of Blue* (1959). He continued to play in trios and compose and eventually won a Grammy in 1981 for his last album, titled *We Will Meet Again*. In total, he won 7 Grammys and received a remarkable 31 nominations.

'Five' - New Jazz Conceptions (1956)

'One for Helen' - Bill Evans at Town Hall (1966)

'Funkallero' - The Bill Evans Album (1971)

"The piano keys are black and white but they sound like a million colors in your mind."
– Maria Cristina Mena

LENNIE TRISTANO (1919–78)

He performed with jazz greats Charlie Parker, saxophonist Lee Konitz and drummer Roy Haynes, but he was also well known as one of the first teachers to teach jazz with a unique structure. He taught musicians who would go on to have long and successful careers, including bassist Charles Mingus, saxophonist Phil Woods and guitarist Joe Satriani.

RED GARLAND (1923–84)

Some of Garland's most important work came in a three-year period playing in the Miles Davis Quintet. Garland's block chord style can be heard on many famous recordings with saxophonists John Coltrane, Art Pepper and Sonny Rollins.

AHMAD JAMAL (born 1930)

Art Tatum called Jamal a 'coming great' when he heard Jamal play at age 14. His use of time and space was different from the quick tempos that many others were playing at the time, and his style helped to influence jazz pianists such as McCoy Tyner, Bill Evans and Herbie Hancock.

TOO MANY HANDS!

The world record for the most amount of people playing a piano at the same time is 88, set on 19 August 2019 in Cambridge, England. The project included 10 universities and 2500 primary school children from across the country.

They even have their own Twitter account!

Q10: Which pianist once had an exhibition boxing match with middleweight champion Sugar Ray Robinson?
a) Bill Evans   b) Earl Hines
c) Wynton Kelly   d) Red Garland

HARD BOP

HORACE SILVER
(1928–2014)
Norwalk, Connecticut, U.S.A.

Silver's mother was a singer in a church choir, which may have had a big impact on the music he went on to compose and record. He learned about folk music from Cape Verde from his father who, as a young man, moved to the United States. In school, young Horace played the saxophone and piano, but after focusing on the piano, it wasn't long before he found himself on tour performing with saxophonist Stan Getz.

As his reputation grew, he recorded with saxophonists Coleman Hawkins, Lou Donaldson, and with Miles Davis during the 1950s. With Art Blakey, Silver set up the Jazz Messengers and, in 1955, recorded one of his biggest hits, *The Preacher*. He later left to set up his own quintet with saxophonist Hank Mobley.

Silver continued to write and perform with that band until the early 1960s, recording his best known album, *Song for My Father*, in 1965. He became well known as a composer, and many of his songs have become jazz standards. Silver was awarded a United States Congress Certificate of Special Congressional Recognition in 2003.

Did you know?
The Horace Silver Foundation was set up by Silver to give scholarships to jazz musicians.

'Nica's Dream' - Horace-Scope (1960)

'Psychedelic Sally' - Serenade To A Soul Sister (1968)

'Soul Searchin'' - Total Response (1972)

TOMMY FLANAGAN
(1930–2001)
Detroit, Michigan, U.S.A.

Flanagan started his musical journey playing the clarinet but quickly decided that the piano was the instrument for him. Early in life, he was influenced by Bud Powell, Nat King Cole and Art Tatum, and while still a teenager, he played with Charlie Parker a couple of times in his hometown. To avoid being sent to war (the Korean War), he joined an army show for a year, but eventually he was sent to Korea for two years.

After moving to New York in 1956, along with saxophonist Sonny Rollins, he recorded one of the most important jazz albums, *Saxophone Colossus*. He went on to play with Ella Fitzgerald and trombonist J.J Johnson before recording such landmark jazz albums as *Giant Steps* with John Coltrane in 1959, and *The Incredible Jazz Guitar of Wes Montgomery* in 1960. During the 1970s and 80s, he continued to perform and record with legends like Ella Fitzgerald and Tony Bennett to name a few. He was awarded the Danish Jazzpur Prize in 1993 for his live album *Flanagan's Shenanigans*. Flanagan was nominated for five Grammy Awards but, unfortunately, never won.

'Dalarna' - Overseas (1957)

'Angel Eyes' - Angel Eyes (1961)

'Oleo' - Eclypso (1977)

HAROLD MABERN
(1936–2019)
Memphis, Tennessee, U.S.A.

After starting his musical journey on the drums, Mabern switched to the piano, but he was unable to fulfill his dream of attending the American Conservatory of Music because his parents couldn't afford it. His father worked hard to save around $60 to buy Mabern a piano. He learnt how to play jazz from private lessons, listening to Ahmad Jamal and practicing intensely for several years.

He moved to New York in 1959 and immediately replaced Tommy Flanagan playing for trumpeter Harry Edison. In the 1960s, he went on to perform with Roy Haynes, Miles Davis, Sarah Vaughan and released his first album, *A Few Miles From Memphis,* in 1968. He also worked as a teacher in New Jersey from 1981 to 2017, and he had a big impact on many musicians who studied with him.

'When You Look Into Your Eyes' - A Season of Ballads (1992)

'Lazybird' - Philadelphia Bound (1995)

'Inner Glimpse' - To Love and Be Loved (2017)

Did you know?
Flanagan played his solo so badly on the original *Giant Steps* recording that a few years later, he recorded an album called *Giant Steps* and played it again — this time perfectly!

MCCOY TYNER
(1938–2020)
Philadelphia, Pennsylvania, U.S.A.

Tyner started playing the piano when he was 13. Some of his childhood friends included trumpeter Lee Morgan and pianist Bobby Timmons. And imagine young McCoy's suprise when the great Bud Powell moved into his neighbourhood!

He began playing as a professional at 22, along with trumpeter Art Farmer and saxophonist Benny Golson, and he then joined John Coltrane's quartet that same year. Tyner played on Coltrane's infamous album, *My Favourite Things*, in 1961, and on a few of Coltrane's other important albums, including *Crescent* (1964) and A Love Supreme (1965). In 1967, he began to record his own music and experimented with different styles and instruments — he even played the koto and flute on his album *Sahara* (1972).

In a career ranging over six decades, he has played with musicians such as saxophonist Wayne Shorter, trumpeter Freddie Hubbard and even Coltrane's son, saxophonist Ravi Coltrane. In 2005, he was awarded an honorary degree from Berklee College of Music to add to his five Grammy wins and twelve nominations!

'There Is No Greater Love' - Inception (1962)

'When Sunny Gets Blue' - Today and Tomorrow (1964)

'Passion Dance' (Live) - Passion Dance (1978)

HERBIE HANCOCK
(born 1940)
Chicago, Illinois, U.S.A.

Like many other pianists, Hancock started playing classical music as a child and even performed with the Chicago Symphony Orchestra when he was only 11. After leaving college, he worked with saxophonist Coleman Hawkins and trumpeter Donald Byrd, and a couple of years later recorded his first album, *Takin' Off* (1962). Miles Davis heard the album and hired Hancock for his band with bassist Ron Carter, drummer Tony Williams and saxophonist Wayne Shorter.

He continued to work with other musicians and record his own music during the 1960s with such albums as *Speak Like a Child* (1968) and *The Prisoner* (1969). In 1973, he started a band called The Headhunters, and their first album, *Head Hunters*, was a big success that same year. Hancock experimented with technology and used vocoders and syntheziers in a lot of his music from 1978.

In 1986, he won an Academy Award for Original Music Score for the film *'Round Midnight*, in which he also played a role. As of 2020, he has won 14 Grammy Awards, has a star on the Hollywood Walk of Fame, and the music video for his tune *Rockit* (1983) was named 10th greatest video by VH1 in 2001.

On 6th October 2018, the Blüthner Piano Group played the Rimsky-Korsakow 'Radezky March' on 666 pianos in China!

'Cantaloupe Island' - Empyrean Isles (1964)

'Chameleon' - Head Hunters (1973)

'Actual Proof' - Thrust (1974)

CHICK COREA
(born 1941)
Chelsea, Massachusetts, U.S.A.

'500 Miles High' - Light as a Feather (1973)

'Spain' - Light as a Feather (1973)

'My One And Only Love' - Now He Sings, Now He Sobs (2002)

Corea's father was a jazz trumpeter, and he started learning the piano when he was about 4. He explored both jazz and classical music and released his first album, *Tones for Joan's Bones*, in 1966. Corea played on *Spaces* in 1970, which is said to have been one of the first jazz fusion albums. He joined Miles Davis's band in 1968 after Herbie Hancock left, and recorded a few albums with him including *In A Silent Way* (1969) and *Bitches Brew* (1970).

He recorded a couple of solo albums before recording one of his most famous albums, *Light as a Feather*, in 1973. By then, his music contained elements of Latin and rock music, and Corea was playing synthesizers as well as the piano. He recorded two albums and performed as a duo with Herbie Hancock in the late 1970s, playing each other's music and some classical pieces, too. He has won 23 Grammys and been nominated 65 times!

KEITH JARRETT
(born 1945)
Allentown, Pennsylvania, U.S.A.

Jarrett was a prodigy who appeared on a TV show he when he was only 5. At 7, he gave a classical piano recital including two of his compositions. He became interested in jazz and was influenced by listening to Dave Brubeck amongst others.

Jarrett studied at Berklee College of Music and then moved to New York where he joined Art Blakey's Jazz Messengers. He started to record his own music from 1967 and got a big break when Miles Davis made him a part of his band in the early 1970s. He has recorded many solo albums, but the most famous was *The Köln Concert* (1975), which is the best-selling piano album and best-selling solo jazz album of all time! He has also recorded classical albums and written for orchestras and other ensembles.

In 1983, he formed a trio with drummer Jack DeJohnette and bass player Gary Peacock. They recorded a few albums, the first was called *Standards, Volume 1*. They continued to tour and record together until 2014. In 2003, Jarrett became the first person to win the Polar Music Prize for classical and contemporary music. He is also well known for making strange noises when he plays!

'So Tender' - Standards, Vol.2 (1983)

'All the Things' - Tribute (1990)

'The Wind' - Paris Concert (1990)

Q11: Which hit TV show has Keith Jarrett's music been featured in?
a) Game Of Thrones b) The Wire
c) Breaking Bad
d) The Sopranos

KENNY DREW (1928–93)

In his long career, Drew recorded with musicians like drummer Buddy Rich, saxophonist Lester Young and on one of John Coltrane's most famous albums, *Blue Train* (1958). He moved to Copenhagen, Denmark, in 1964, and when he died, had a street named after him — 'Kenny Drews Vej'.

JOE ZAWINUL (1932–2007)

Zawinul was born in Austria but moved to the United States in 1959 and spent a lot of time playing with saxophonist Cannonball Adderley in the 1960s. He co-founded a band called Weather Report with saxophonist Wayne Shorter and bassist Miroslav Vitous, which went on to win many awards and become recognized as one of the most important jazz fusion bands of all time.

ABDULLAH IBRAHIM (1934–)

Born in Cape Town, South Africa, Ibrahim recorded with Duke Ellington in the early 1960s and moved to New York a few years later to study and perform with saxophonists Ornette Coleman, Pharaoh Sanders and John Coltrane. He was awarded the South African Music Lifetime Achievement Award in 2007.

CEDAR WALTON (1934–2013)

Walton performed and recorded with many musicians, such as trumpeter Donald Byrd, vocalist Etta James and the Jazz Messengers. He recorded almost 50 albums as a leader or co-leader.

The fastest descending chromatic scale (unofficially) was performed by Schacht21 (YouTube user name). He played it in 5.84 seconds in 2012!

CONTEMPORARY

GEORGE DUKE
(1946–2013)
San Rafael, California, U.S.A.

George Duke was one of the most versatile piano players of all time. One of his earliest musical experiences was seeing Duke Ellington perform, which inspired him to start taking piano lessons. Even though he graduated from college focusing on the trombone, he continued playing the piano and was soon afterwards recording his own albums and performing with guitarist Frank Zappa and Cannonball Adderley.

Duke recorded a lot of jazz-inspired pop and funk music. One of his best-known albums, which also features him singing, is titled *Brazilian Love Affair* (1979). His song 'Sweet Baby' (1981) went to number 19 on the pop charts and was the first single of his collaboration with bassist Stanley Clarke. This experience led him to produce music for singers like Anita Baker, Barry Manilow and The Pointer Sisters, as well as recording *The Gospel According To Jazz Chapter I, II & III* with saxophonist Kirk Whalum. For many years, he was the music director for the Soul Train awards, and he produced a Grammy Award-winning album for his cousin, vocalist Dianne Reeves in 2000. He won an Edison Lifetime Achievement Award in 2005.

Q12:

Which pop star did George Duke play with?

a) Prince b) Alexander O'Neal

c) George Michael d) Michael Jackson

'Reach Out' - Guardian Of The Light (1983)

'My Piano' - Face The Music (2002)

'For All We Know' - In A Mellow Tone (2006)

Q: What do you get when you drop a piano on an army base?

A: A flat major!

BRAD MEHLDAU
(born 1970)
Jacksonville, Florida, U.S.A.

Mehldau became interested in jazz around age 14 by listening to pianists like Oscar Peterson and Keith Jarrett. By the time he graduated from The New School in 1993, he was already touring and had even performed with one of his teachers, the legendary drummer Jimmy Cobb. He worked with saxophonist Joshua Redman starting from 1992, and went on to record with both Redman and saxophonist Mark Turner in 1994.

His recordings *Introducing Brad Mehldau* (1995) and *Live at the Village Vanguard: The Art of the Trio Volume Two* (1997) helped develop his reputation. You can hear his classical background in much of his music, and that skill has led him to score film soundtracks.

Mehldau often covers pop tunes by artists like Radiohead and The Beatles with his unique style, in addition to composing music for his favourite poetry, some of it in German. To date he has won seven *DownBeat* Readers Poll piano awards, the 2006 Miles Davis Prize, and has been nominated for nine Grammy Awards.

'When It Rains' - Largo (2002)

'John Boy' - Highway Rider (2010)

'The Nearness Of You' - Nearness (2016)

ROBERT GLASPER
(born 1978)
Houston, Texas, U.S.A.

Glasper has been credited with introducing jazz music to young audiences since 2009 with his albums *Double Booked and Black Radio* (2012). Growing up, he played in many churches, and his music is often inspired by the gospel chords and phrasing he developed there.

Before recording his first album, *Mood,* in 2004, he performed with trumpeters Roy Hargrove and Terrance Blanchard. Glasper often plays a combination of piano and keyboards, sometimes both at the same time! He is well known for mixing jazz and hip-hop and has worked with rappers such as Jay-Z, Mos Def and Common. He played keyboards and piano on the hit album by Kendrick Lamar, *To Pimp A Butterfly*, in 2015. And his albums *Black Radio* (2012) and *Black Radio 2* (2013) featured many R&B and neo soul singers such as Erykah Badu and Jill Scott, which helped to increase his appeal to non-jazz fans.

Glasper composed, arranged and produced music for the 2015 film *Miles Ahead* about one of his influences, Miles Davis. He has won three Grammy Awards, including Best R&B Album for *Black Radio* in 2013.

'Jelly's Da Beener' - Canvas (2005)

'F.T.B.' - In My Element (2007)

'So Beautiful' - Covered (2015)

ELAINE ELIAS (born 1960)

Elias is a Brazilian pianist who has performed and recorded with bassist Stanley Clarke, saxophonist Michael Brecker and vocalist Gilberto Gil. Her album *Made in Brazil* (2015) won a Grammy for the Best Latin Jazz Album, and she won a Latin Grammy in 2017 for her album *Dance of Time*.

MICHEL PETRUCCIANI (1962–99)

Petrucciani suffered from a disease that caused him to grew to only three feet tall, and he had a lot of pain in his arms throughout his whole life. He decided he wanted to play the piano after watching Duke Ellington on TV. His disability didn't stop him from recording many albums in the 1980s, including *Estate* (1982) and *Power of Three* (1986) with saxophonist Wayne Shorter and guitarist Jim Hall.

JULIAN JOSEPH (born 1966)

London born Joseph is well known as a pianist and jazz educator. He has performed and recorded with saxophonists Jean Toussaint and Courtney Pine as well as drummer Billy Cobham. He is the founder of the London-based Julian Joseph Jazz Academy, and he has helped to create jazz study programs worldwide.

103 musicians played the same piano in Japan on 22 April 2012 by playing Beethoven's Ode To Joy for 20 minutes! They had to rotate who played so everyone had a turn!

HARRY CONNICK JR (born 1967)

Connick is one of the best-selling artists of all time and has won three Grammy Awards so far. He learned piano from Ellis Marsalis Jr and performed with a 96-year-old Eubie Blake when he was 9! His album *Only You* (2004) reached number one on the *Billboard* Top Jazz Album chart and has starred in Hollywood movies such as *Independence Day* (1996) alongside Will Smith, and he has appeared for three seasons as a judge on *American Idol*.

HIROMI UEHARA (born 1979)

Hiromi met pianist Chick Corea when she was 17, and he invited her to play with him the next day! She studied at Berklee College of Music and was introduced to Ahmad Jamal by one of her teachers. Her first album won a Jazz Album of the Year Award. In 2016, her album *Spark* went to #1 on the U.S. *Billboard* Jazz Album chart. So far, Uehara has performed with bassist Stanley Clarke, drummer Lenny White, Chick Corea and many others.

JOEY ALEXANDER (born 2003)

Alexander taught himself to play jazz and became an international sensation, playing at Jazz at Lincoln Center in 2014 when he was only 10! His first album was released when he was 11, and it was nominated for a 2016 Grammy. So far in his young career, he has played with musicians like saxophonist Chris Potter, bassist Larry Grenadier, and performed in front of two U.S. Presidents.

ROCK

LITTLE RICHARD
(1932-2020)
Macon, Georgia, U.S.A.

His official name was Richard Wayne Penniman, but he was given the nickname Little Richard because of how small he was! Like many black musicians at the time, he started singing in church, but he actually started playing the saxophone when he was in school. His very religious family was not very happy when he started learning the piano and singing non-religious music.

Little Richard performed across America with many musicians, which led him to start recording his own music. His first hit, *Tutti Frutti* (1955), was one of his biggest and reached No. 2 on the *Billboard* Rhythm and Blues chart, selling more than one million copies. He was so popular that two of the biggest rock stars at the time Elvis Presley and Bill Haley recorded some of Richard's music in 1956. By 1959, he had 26 songs in the top 40 pop and R&B singles charts.

He became very religious and recorded a gospel album, *King of the Gospel Singers* (1962). His career went up and down from there with a few appearances on TV and shows in London, Atlantic City and New York.

Little Richard has influenced musicians like Elton John, Mick Jagger and Bruno Mars, and is recognized as a pioneer of rock and roll. He was inducted into the Rock and Roll Hall of Fame in 1986, has a star on the Hollywood Walk of Fame and a Grammy Lifetime Achievement Award.

'Slippin' and Slidin'' - Little Richard And His Band (1956)

'Long Tall Sally' - Here's Little Richard (1957)

'Good Golly Miss Molly' - Little Richard (1958)

JERRY LEE LEWIS
(born 1935)
Ferriday, Louisiana, U.S.A.

Lewis was born into a poor family and his family had to put themselves into debt to buy him a piano. He started to record at 19 and travelled to Tennessee to play on recordings with Johnny Cash, Carl Perkins and Elvis Presley. His biggest hit was 'Great Balls of Fire' (1957), which became one of the best-selling singles of all time. A few of his songs contained lyrics that seemed risqué at the time, which many religious people found very offensive!

In 1964, Lewis recorded *Live at the Star Club, Hamburg* (1964), which has been called one of the greatest live rock and roll albums ever. In the 1970s, he had many top 10 hits including 'Since I Met You Baby' (1970) and 'Sometimes A Memory Ain't Enough' (1973).

Lewis was in the first group of performers to be inducted into the Rock and Roll Hall of Fame (along with Little Richard) and was given a star on the Hollywood Walk of Fame in 1989. In 2005, he was given a Lifetime Achievement Award from The Recording Academy.

'Whole Lot of Shakin' Going On' (1958)

'Another Place, Another Time' (1968)

'One Minute Past Eternity' (1969)

Did you know?
Lewis was famous for running his fingers up and down the piano,
and often kicked the piano stool over and played standing up.

BILLY JOEL
(born 1949)
The Bronx, New York, U.S.A.

Joel dropped out of school to concentrate on his music career, and, at 22, released his first album, *Cold Spring Harbor* (1971). One of his most well-known songs, 'Piano Man', appeared on his 1973 album of the same name. He often performs it as an audience sing-along at his live shows.

Joel released many more albums over the next 30 years, and he toured as a duo with Elton John from 1994 until 2010. In 2001, he released an album called *Fantasies & Delusions*, which featured pianist Hyung-ki Joo playing Joel's classical compositions.

One of the most successful musicians of all time, he has sold more than 150 million records globally, has won five Grammys and has a star on the Hollywood Walk of Fame. The 18th July 2018 was even named Billy Joel Day in New York! No wonder his nickname is 'Piano Man'!

'Uptown Girl' - An Innocent Man (1983)

'We Didn't Start the Fire' - Storm Front (1989)

'Everybody Loves You Now' - 12 Gardens Live (2006)

> **Did you know?**
> Hornsby's song 'Just The Way It Is' (1986) was sampled by 2Pac in 1998 for the song 'Changes'.

BRUCE HORNSBY
(born 1954)
Williamsburg, Virginia, U.S.A.

Hornsby studied music in college and moved to Los Angeles with his brother in 1980 to write music for 20th Century Fox. In 1984, he formed his own band, Bruce Hornsby and the Range, which stayed together for seven years. Their album *The Way It Is* (1986) sold millions of copies. He has continued to record and write hits for many musicians, including Bob Dylan, Stevie Nicks and saxophonist Wayne Shorter.

Hornsby played piano and accordion many times with the Grateful Dead in the early 1990s, and in 1993, he released his first solo album, *Harbor Lights.* As his piano playing became more versatile, he would often combine elements of classical, jazz, folk and bluegrass music in his solo piano concerts. In 2007, he released a bluegrass album, *Ricky Skaggs & Bruce Hornsby*, and a jazz album, Camp Meeting, which featured tunes by Bud Powell, Thelonious Monk and Keith Jarrett.

Hornsby has also worked a lot with filmmaker Spike Lee, including scoring the music for his Netflix series *She's Gotta Have It* (2017).

'The Valley Road' - Scenes from the Southside (1988)

'Spider Fingers' - Hot House (1995)

'Hooray For Tom' - Halcyon Days (2004)

MARC COHN
(born 1959)
Cleveland, Ohio, U.S.A.

Cohn taught himself to play the piano in college and moved to New York to follow his dreams. He played piano with singer Tracy Chapman on her album *Crossroads* (1989) before recording his first solo album in 1991, *Marc Cohn*. His most successful song, 'Walking in Memphis', was on that album, and he received two Grammy nominations and won the 1992 Grammy for Best New Artist. Since then, he has worked with artists like Bonnie Raitt, India.Arie and the Blind Boys of Alabama.

Q13: Which pianist married his 13-year-old cousin?
a) Rick Wakeman **b)** Billy Joel
c) Jerry Lee Lewis **d)** Bruce Hornsby

Did you know?
Marc Cohn was shot in the head in 2005 but survived almost unharmed!

'True Companion' -
Marc Cohn (1991)

'The Thing's We've Handed Down' - The
Rainy Season (1993)

'After Midnight' - Listening Booth: 1970 (2010)

KEITH EMERSON (1944–2016)

Emerson was influenced by pianists like Dave Brubeck, Little Richard and Jerry Lee Lewis before he became a member of the supergroup Emerson, Lake and Palmer. *Contemporary Keyboard* magazine voted him Overall Best Keyboardist for five years in a row (1975-80).

BILLY PRESTON (1946–2006)

Preston worked with many famous musicians and bands including the Beatles, Ray Charles, Little Richard and The Rolling Stones. He won two Grammy Awards in 1973.

TIMOTHY JAMES RICE-OXLEY (born 1976)

Rice-Oxley grew up hating his classical music lessons but learnt how to play by listening to bands like The Beatles, Blondie and The Smiths. He has been part of the British band Keane since 1995.

RICK WAKEMAN (born 1979)

Wakeman, a longtime member of the legendary band Yes, has worked with artists such as Elton John and David Bowie and wrote music for a movie about Franz Liszt called *Lisztomania* (1975). He has recorded more than 90 solo albums!

HIP-HOP*

'C.R.E.A.M.' - WU-TANG CLAN (1993)

C.R.E.A.M. was named as the sixth-greatest hip-hop song of all time by the BBC in 2019. It appears on their first album, *Enter the Wu-Tang (36 Chambers)*, which is also considered one of the most influential hip-hop albums of all time. (3:22-3:39)

'THE WORLD IS YOURS' - NAS (1994)

The sample that you hear through the whole song was taken from a tune by the Ahmad Jamal Trio, 'I Love Music' (1970). This tune appears on Nas's classic album *Illmatic* (1994). (0:00-0:21)

'AHMAD IMPRESSES ME' - J DILLA (1996)

Internationally respected producer J Dilla sampled Ahmad Jamal's tune 'The Awakening' (1970) to put this beat together. (0:21-0:43)

'I AIN'T MAD AT CHA' - 2PAC FT. DANNY BOY (1996)

The piano sample was taken from a song called 'A Dream' (1983) by a soul group called DeBarge. This song appeared on 2pac's fourth album, *All Eyez on Me* (1996). (4:23-4:35)

'STILL D.R.E.' - DR. DRE FT. SNOOP DOGG (1999)

One of Dr. Dre's most famous tunes, it has appeared in video games, TV shows and movies since it was released. It was the first single on his album *2001* (1999), which has sold more than 7 million copies. (4:06-4:17)

'I CAN' - NAS (2002)

Taken from Nas's sixth album called *God's Son* (2002), the main piano riff actually comes from the opening of Beethoven's famous 'Für Elise' (1810). (0:00-0:27)

* Time stamps show the important piano parts of each song. The full songs may not be appropriate for some age groups.

'MY BLOCK' - SCARFACE (2002)

This was the lead single from the album *The Fix* (2002) and is sampled from a song called 'Be Real Black For Me' (1971) by Donny Hathaway and Roberta Flack. (0:00-0:11)

'HEARD 'EM SAY' - KANYE WEST FT. ADAM LEVINE (2005)

This was originally from a song by Natalie Cole called 'Someone That I Used to Love' (1980). (0:10-0:28)

'HOMECOMING' - KANYE WEST FT. CHRIS MARTIN (2007)

This tune appeared on Kanye's album *Graduation* (2007) and won a Grammy in 2008 for Best Rap album. The music video was nominated at the 2008 MTV Awards for Best Hip-Hop Video. (0:00-0:25)

'BLACK' - DAVE (2019)

This song reached the top 10 on the UK R&B charts and was part of the album *Psychodrama* (2019), which won the Album of the Year at the Brit Awards, and the Mercury Prize in 2019. (0:00-0:35)

JAMES POYSER (born 1967)

SCOTT STORCH (born 1973)

88-KEYS (born 1976)

SAM BARSH (born 1981)

CHLOE FLOWER (born 1985)

The oldest Grammy winner was a pianist called Pinetop Perkins who won the award when he was 95!!

GOSPEL

RICHARD SMALLWOOD
(born 1948)
Atlanta, Georgia, U.S.A.

Smallwood is one of the most recognizable and influential gospel artists of all time. He grew up in church and was always surrounded by music. He helped to start a choir at Howard University and wrote a song called 'I Love the Lord', which was recorded by singer Whitney Houston for the 1996 film *The Preacher's Wife*. Smallwood has performed for three U.S. Presidents, and he has worked with many artists including singer Chaka Khan and producer Quincy Jones. He has won 10 Stellar awards and been nominated for 8 Grammys.

You're never too young! Ethan Bortnick became the youngest person to headline his own concert tour in 2009 when he was just 9 years old!

'Center Of My Joy' - Textures (1987)

'Total Praise' - Healing Live In Detroit (1999)

'Trust Me' - Promises (2011)

KEN BURTON
(born 1970)
Croydon, London, UK

Ken Burton is a London-based pianist, composer, arranger and choir leader. He has led the London Adventist Chorale for more than 15 years and has appeared with them on the BBC TV shows *Songs of Praise* and on *EastEnders*. He regularly appears on other TV programs such as The X Factor (UK and U.S. versions) and *Britain's Got Talent*. He has arranged and performed with artists such as Beyoncé, Robbie Williams and will.i.am, and performed at Buckingham Palace for Queen Elizabeth II's Golden Jubilee in 2002. He also led the Voquality Singers who sung on the award-winning Marvel movie *Black Panther* in 2018.

'Love Without End' - Love Without End (2010)

'We Know Not The Hour' - Advent Songs, Vol. 1 (2011)

'Nobody Knows the Trouble I See' - Sounds of Gospel (2015)

JASON WHITE
Los Angeles, California, U.S.A.

White is well known and highly respected not only in gospel music, but in pop, too. He has played and produced for many gospel artists including Andrae Crouch, Kurt Carr, and Mary Mary, as well as other artists like Tim McGraw, Brian McKnight, Aretha Franklin and P. Diddy. He is also the choir director for Kanye West's Sunday Service Gospel Choir which released their album *Jesus Is Born* in 2019.

'Emmanuel' - Norman Hutchins (2001)

'Oh Give Thanks' - Judith Christie McAllister (2001)

'I Try'- Mary Mary (2002)

MIKE BEREAL
Pasadena, California, U.S.A.

Bereal has been working in the gospel industry for many years as a composer, performer and producer. He has performed and worked with artists like Juanita Bynum, Kim Burrell, Kirk Franklin and Dr. Judith McAllister, as well as being nominated for multiple Stellar Awards.

'I'm Still Here' - Dorinda Clark Cole (2002)

'It's About Time for a Miracle' - Beverly Crawford (2010)

'How Great Is Our God' - Judith Christie McAllister (2011)

THOMAS WHITFIELD (1954-92)

Whitfield was a highly influential pianist, singer and director, who has influenced many gospel artists including Richard Smallwood, Donald Lawrence and John P. Kee. He was involved with many Grammy nominated songs and albums, and was awarded the James Cleveland Award in 1999.

KEVIN BOND (born 1964)

Bond has recorded and performed with many top gospel artists such as Walter Hawkins, Donald Lawrence and Bishop T.D. Jakes. He even produced a song for the soundtrack of the film *The Prince of Egypt (Inspirational)*, in 1998!

AYRON LEWIS

Lewis has recorded and performed with vocalists such as Kurt Carr, Shirley Caesar and Beverley Crawford.

SHAUN MARTIN

Martin is a multiple-award-winning piano and keyboard player, having worked with Kirk Franklin, Fred Hammond and Tamela Mann. He has also won Grammys as a keyboardist in the jazz fusion band Snarky Puppy.

On 27th January 2019, 553 pairs of hands played in the largest four-hand ensemble in China led by pianist Lang Lang.

AARON LINDSEY

Lindsey has won six Grammys and multiple Dove and Stellar awards. He has worked with vocalists Erica Campbell, Israel & New Breed, and Marvin Sapp.

'PRECIOUS LORD, TAKE MY HAND' - THOMAS DORSEY (1932)

Dorsey wrote this song after a major life tragedy. His wife and son died during childbirth, and that emotion was a strong influence for him to write this song.

'AS THE DEER' - MARTIN J. NYSTROM (1981)

This song has been recorded by many Christian artists in many different languages all over the world.

'ALABASTER BOX' - DR. JANICE SJOSTRAND (2001)

Though written by Dr. Janice Sjostrand, it was recorded by Cece Winans and won a Dove Award in 2001.

'I CAN ONLY IMAGINE' - MERCYME (2001)

One of the best-selling Christian songs of all time, it was made into a movie by the same title in 2018.

'I NEED YOU NOW' - SMOKIE NORFUL (2002)

This is one of Norful's most famous songs. It is taken from the album of the same name.

The biggest piano ever was made by Daniel Czapiewski in Poland in 2010. It was 6.07meters long, 2.49 meters wide and 1.92 meters high! It also had 156 keys!!

'IMAGINE ME' - KIRK FRANKLIN (2005)

This song appeared on Franklin's album *Hero* in 2005 and won the Grammy Award for Best Gospel Song in 2007.

'NEVER WOULD HAVE MADE IT' - MARVIN SAPP (2007)

This song has been streamed more than 12 million times on Spotify and was written in tribute to Sapp's late father.

'TAKE ME TO THE KING' - TAMELA MANN FT. KIRK FRANKLIN (2012)

Written and produced by Kirk Franklin, it was a big success and sold more than 1 million copies in the United States. It appears on Mann's album, *Best Days* (2012).

'BLINDED BY YOUR GRACE PT.1' - STORMZY (2017)

Although Stormzy is a rapper, this song was included in his first album, *Gang Signs & Prayer*.

'EVERY HOUR' - KANYE WEST FT. SUNDAY SERVICE CHOIR (2019)

West is not normally known for producing gospel music, but he released the album *Jesus Is King*, which went to number one on the Top Gospel Album charts.

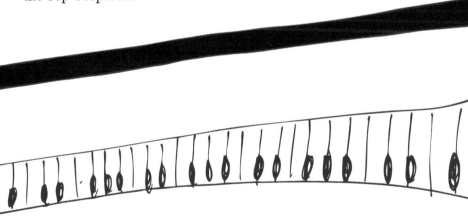

POP

GREG PHILLINGANES
(born 1956)
Detroit, Michigan, U.S.A.

Phillinganes started learning the piano by ear when he was just 2, and he began formal piano lessons when he was about 6. He was inspired by keyboard players like Herbie Hancock and Chick Corea, and he joined Stevie Wonder's band, Wonderlove, when he was 18. He played on some of Stevie's hit songs, including 'Isn't She Lovely' (1976) and 'Contusion' (1976), which led him work with Michael Jackson and The Jackson 5.

Phillinganes released his first album, *Significant Gains,* in 1981, and followed it up with Pulse in 1984. He has worked with musicians like Paul McCartney, vocalist Joan Armatrading and guitarist George Benson, and he won a Primetime Emmy for Outstanding Music Direction in 2015 for his work on Stevie Wonder's *Songs In The Key Of Life* Grammy Tribute special.

'Havana' - Kenny G (1996)

'24K Magic' - Bruno Mars (2016)

'This Christmas Day' - Jessie J (2018)

JOHN LEGEND
(born 1978)
Springfield, Ohio, U.S.A.

Did you know?
John Legend is the first black man to win an Emmy, Grammy, Oscar and a Tony in his career.

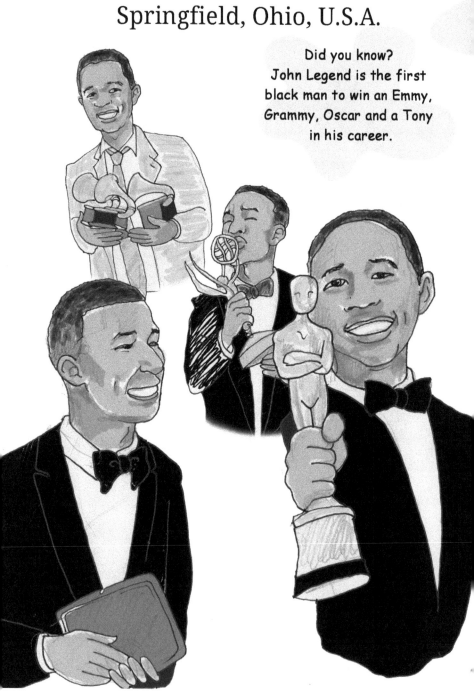

'Ordinary People' - Get Lifted (2005)

'So High' - Get Lifted (2005)

'All Of Me' - Love In The Future (2013)

Legend grew up in a musical family and was already performing with his local church choir at 4. He started playing the piano at 7, and in college, he performed in a few different bands. He even played piano on Ms. Lauryn Hill's song 'Everything is Everything' (1999).

Legend's first album, *Get Lifted*, was released in 2004, and it won a Grammy in 2006 for best R&B album. The lead single from it, 'Ordinary People', reached number one on the UK R&B charts in 2012. He has performed at sporting events including Wrestlemania XXIV, the 2006 NBA All-Star Game and Super Bowl XL. In total, he has won 33 awards including 10 Grammys, 2 American Music Awards and 2 BET awards. As a vocalist, he has featured on tunes with The Black-Eyed Peas, Kanye West and David Guetta.

The world's smallest piano is only 25 cm wide, 18cm tall and 33cm deep!

Alicia Keys
(born 1981)
New York City, New York, U.S.A.

Keys started playing the piano at 6 after hearing her mum play jazz albums at home on Sunday mornings. She learned and listened to classical music by composers such as Mozart and Chopin. As she grew older, she explored singers like Curtis Mayfield, Nina Simone and Barbra Streisand and formed a band with a friend from school.

Despite a few bad experiences in the music industry, Keys continued writing and recording until she released her first album, *Songs in A minor* (2001). It won her five Grammy Awards in 2002, and she followed it with *The Diary of Alicia Keys* (2003), which won her three more Grammys. She is a global superstar and has inspired others like Bruno Mars, Adele and James Bay. Keys has sold more than 30 million albums worldwide and won a total of 15 Grammy Awards.

'Fallin" - Songs In A Minor (2001)

'If I Ain't Got You' - The Diary Of Alicia Keys (2003)

'No One' - As I Am (2007)

The piano riff at the beginning of 'A Song For You' (Leon Russell, 1970) is featured in Alicia Keys' 2003 song 'You Don't Know My Name'.

The piano that Lennon used to record this song was bought by pop star George Michael for £1.45 million($2.37 million). He later donated it to a museum.

LET IT BE - THE BEATLES (1970)

John Lennon and Paul McCartney wrote this, one of most-popular Beatles songs, which was inspired by McCartney's mother. McCartney himself played the piano. It was ranked as the 20th best song of all time on the Rolling Stone 500 Greatest Songs of All Time list.

IMAGINE - JOHN LENNON (1971)

Lennon played the piano on this iconic song. It won a Grammy Hall of Fame Award and Rolling Stone ranked it as the third greatest song of all time (out of 500).

BOHEMIAN RHAPSODY - QUEEN (1975)

This song is easily one of the most streamed and played songs of all time, and it is often talked about as one of the greatest of all time. It has sold approximately 6 million copies worldwide.

EASY - COMMODORES (1977)

Easy was written by the lead singer of The Commodores, Lionel Richie, and was a top ten hit worldwide. It was a softer song to the band's normal sound, but it remains one of their most-recognizable.

A THOUSAND MILES - VANESSA CARLTON (2002)

Carlton's first and most successful single so far. It won a VH1 award in 2002 and was nominated for three Grammys. It reached number one on the U.S. Top 40 charts and was featured in the movie *White Chicks* in 2004.

Did you know?
The same piano was used to record 'Bohemian Rhapsody' and Paul McCartney's 'Hey Jude' (1968).

CLOCKS - COLDPLAY (2003)

This is one of Coldplay's most famous songs and it won a Grammy for Record of the Year in 2004. It has appeared in TV shows and movies including *ER, Family Guy* and *The Wild.* In 2010, *Rolling Stone* magazine ranked this song 490th in their top 500 greatest songs of all time.

SOMEONE LIKE YOU - ADELE (2011)

This song was one of the most popular from Adele's album *21* and was her first number-one single in the UK. The piano was played by her co-writer, Dan Wilson. She received MOBO and Brit Award nominations and won a Grammy for Best Pop Solo Performance.

Q: Where do pianists go on vacation?
A: The Florida Keys!

'Pinetop Boogie Woogie' - Pinetop Is Just Top (1976)

'Look One Yonder's Wall' - Live At 85! (2005)

'How Long Blues' - Pinetop Perkins on the 88's: Love in Chicago (2007)

BLUES

PINETOP PERKINS
(1913–2011)
Austin, Texas, U.S.A.

In the 1930s, 40s and 50s, he played with singer Sonny Boy Williamson and guitarists B.B. King and Earl Hooker. He joined the Muddy Waters band in 1969 and then started the Legendary Blues Band, which had a lot of success. Perkins started a solo career when he was in his 80s and performed and toured around the world. He won a Lifetime Achievement Award Grammy in 2005 and continued playing until he died at age 98!

RAY CHARLES
(1930–2004)
Albany, Georgia, U.S.A.

Charles became interested in the piano at age 3 after hearing pianist Wylie Pitman. Charles became blind at 7 but continued playing the piano by learning how to read Braille music and performing popular songs. Eventually, he moved to Seattle, Washington, to form his own band while arranging music for other musicians, including composer Cole Porter and Dizzy Gillespie.

Charles had a string of hits in the 1950s, including *I've Got a Woman* (1954) (which was sampled by Kanye West in 2005), and 'What'd I Say' (1959). He recorded 'Georgia on My Mind' in 1960, which earned him four Grammy Awards, and then 'Hit the Road Jack' (1961), which won him another Grammy. He is one of the most influential musicians of the 20th century and has been awarded with a star on the Hollywood Walk of Fame, 17 Grammy wins and a Grammy Lifetime Achievement Award. Charles has influenced such singers and musicians as Stevie Wonder, Billy Joel and Aretha Franklin, and a movie made about his life, *Ray*, opened in 2005. He was even put on a U.S. postage stamp in 2013!

'Hallelujah, I Love Her So' - Ray Charles (1957)

'Unchain My Heart' (1961)

'I Can't Stop Loving You' - Modern Sounds in Country and Western Music (1962)

DR. JOHN
(1941–2019)
New Orleans, Louisiana, U.S.A.

Dr. John grew up in a family full of piano players. He mostly played guitar when he was young, but after an injury to his left hand in 1960, the piano became his main instrument. He became a session musician in Los Angeles and worked on music for the singer Cher and guitarist Frank Zappa before becoming a solo artist.

Dr. John was heavily influenced by New Orleans voodoo, and he featured voodoo chants and rhythms in his music. As his influence grew, he worked with the likes of Mick Jagger and Eric Clapton, who appeared on his 1971 album *The Sun, Moon & Herbs*. He performed and collaborated with many musicians throughout his life and his voice appeared in two films for Disney: In 1996, he sang the song 'Cruella de Ville' in *101 Dalmatians*; and in 2009, he performed 'Down in New Orleans' in *The Princess and the Frog*. Dr. John won six Grammy Awards and was inducted into the Rock and Roll Hall of Fame in 2011.

Did you know?
Dr.John performed at the 2014 NBA All-Star Game!

'Iko Iko' - Dr.John's Gumbo (1972)

'Such A Night' - In The Right Place (1973)

'Dear Old Southland' - N'Awlinz Dis, Dat, or D'Udda (2004)

MEADE LUX LEWIS (1905–64)

He was good friends with another pianist, Albert Ammons, and they played together throughout their careers. Lewis was regarded as one of the most important boogie-woogie pianists of his time.

ALBERT AMMONS (1907–49)

Ammons and Meade Lux Lewis used to practise on the same piano together at Ammons's house. He started his own bands, one of which, Rhythm Kings, sold a million copies of their version of *Swanee River Boogie* (1936). When he moved to New York, he performed with clarinetist Benny Goodman and with his son, saxophonist Gene Ammons. He played at U.S. President Harry Truman's inauguration but unfortunately died at age 42. He has influenced pianists such as Errol Garner, Dr. John and Jerry Lee Lewis.

PROFESSOR LONGHAIR (1918–80)

Longhair was well admired by other pianists like Dr. John and Allen Toussaint. The piano he learnt to play on had some keys missing, which gave him a unique style! He recorded tunes like 'Bald Head' (1950) and 'Go to the Mardi Gras' (1959). His style was called 'rhumba boogie' because he combined elements of the blues with various Caribbean influences. He was inducted into the Blues Hall of Fame in 1981 and the Rock and Roll Hall of Fame in 1992.

OTIS SPANN (1930–70)

Spann began playing the piano at 7. He eventually moved from Jackson, Mississippi, to Chicago in order to record as a solo musician. He also worked with singer Howlin' Wolf, guitarist B.B. King and the band Fleetwood Mac. Spann was inducted into the Blues Hall of Fame in 1980.

ALLEN TOUSSAINT (1938–2015)

When he was only 19, he stood in for Fats Domino on Domino's record 'I Want You to Know' (1957) and also started producing music for other artists. He produced a series of hits in the 60s and 70s including the hit 'Lady Marmalade' (1975) and for various singers and musicians, including Otis Redding and Jessie Hill. He was inducted into the Rock and Roll Hall of Fame in 1998 and the Blues Hall of Fame in 2011. U.S. President Barack Obama awarded him the National Medal of Arts in 2013.

MARCIA BALL (born 1949)

Ball was influenced by Fats Domino and Professor Longhair as a child. Performing mainly as a solo artist, she won Best Blues Instrumentalist-Keyboards in 1998, 2005, 2006, 2007 and 2009, and has been nominated for three Grammys.

Did you know? Ball won the Pinetop Perkins Piano Player award at the Blue Music Awards in 2015 and 2019.

The first piano concerto for a cat (thats right, a cat!) was first performed in Lithuania on 5th June 2009. It was composed by Mindaugas Piečaitis who took the notes from a video of a cat named Nora playing the piano on YouTube and Piečaitis wrote the music for the orchestra to accompany her!

'Sinnerman' - Pastel Blues (1965)

'Four Women' - Wild Is The Wind (1966)

'Mr.Bojangles' (Live) - It Is Finished (1974)

SOUL AND R&B
NINA SIMONE
(1933–2003)
Tryon, North Carolina, U.S.A.

Born into a poor family, Simone was playing the piano in her local church at around 4 years old. She studied classical music and performed in her first concert at 12. Her first name was actually Eunice, but chose to perform as Nina Simone because she knew her mother wouldn't approve of her playing non-religious music. Her first album, *Little Blue Girl* (1959), was a success with her both singing and playing a mixture of jazz standards and songs from musicals.

Simone wrote several songs during the Civil Rights era that protested the treatment of African Americans in the southern United States. And she accused the music industry of hurting her career after some of her songs, such as 'I Wish I Knew How It Would Feel to Be Free' (1967) and 'Why? (The King of Love Is Dead)' (1968), were viewed as politically radical. But she continued to perform globally and record in countries such as England, Switzerland and France, creating hits like 'To Be Young, Gifted & Black' (1970).

In 2000, she received a Grammy Hall of Fame Award to go along with her four Grammy nominations, two honorary degrees and Rock and Roll Hall of Fame induction. She has been an influence for many musicians including Elton John, David Bowie and Meshell Ndegeocello.

Sculptor Zenos Frudakis created an 8-foot sculpture of Simone, which is placed at Nina Simone Plaza in Tryon, North Carolina, and even contains some of her ashes.

DONNY HATHAWAY
(1945–1979)
Chicago, Illinois, U.S.A.

Hathaway started singing and playing the piano at a young age in his local church. He studied music at Howard University with a full scholarship, but he didn't finish school as he already had many offers to record and perform! He started as a session musician and played piano for many different musicians, including Aretha Franklin, the Impressions and Curtis Mayfield. His first single, 'The Ghetto, Pt. 1', remains one of his most famous songs.

Hathaway's first album, *Everything Is Everything*, was released in 1970, and his second was a 1972 collaboration with his longtime friend, Roberta Flack, titled *Roberta Flack & Donny Hathaway*. Unfortunately, he struggled with depression, which meant that as the years went by, he performed and recorded less and less. Even though he died at 33, he influenced many singers, including Alicia Keys, Amy Winehouse and Justin Timberlake. Hathaway is on the St. Louis Walk of Fame and was given a Grammy Lifetime Achievement Award in 2019 to go with his other Grammy win in 1973.

'The Ghetto' - Everything Is Everything (1970)

'A Song for You' - Donny Hathaway (1971)

'This Christmas' - Donny Hathaway (1971)

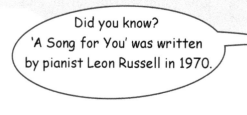

Did you know?
'A Song for You' was written
by pianist Leon Russell in 1970.

134

STEVIE WONDER
(born 1950)
Saginaw, Michigan, U.S.A.

Wonder became blind soon after he was born, but that didn't stop him from learning to play the piano, drums and harmonica when he was really young. The CEO of the famous Motown Record label, Berry Gordy, signed Wonder to a record deal when he was just 11. Only a year later, his first No.1 hit, 'Fingertips', made him the youngest artist to ever top the charts.

His extreme versatility allowed Wonder to play many instruments on some of his biggest hits, like 'Superstition' (1972) 'Living for the City' (1973) and 'Boogie On Reggae Woman' (1974). His first platinum album was *Hotter Than July* (1980), which included the timeless 'Happy Birthday' and 'Master Blaster (Jammin')'.

Wonder has collaborated with many artists, often singing and/or playing harmonica with rapper Busta Rhymes, musicians Sting, India.Arie and vocalist Andrea Bocelli. He has won 25 Grammys (a record for a solo artist), and an Oscar for his 1984 song 'I Just Called To Say I Love You'. He has a star on the Hollywood Walk of Fame and has been inducted into the Rock and Roll Hall of Fame and the Songwriters Hall of Fame.

Did you know? Stevie Wonder's real name is Stevland Morris!

'For Once In My Life' - For Once In My Life (1968)

'Never Dreamed You'd Leave In Summer' - Where I'm Coming From (1971)

'Isn't She Lovely' - Songs In The Key Of Life (1976)

MICHAEL MCDONALD
(born 1952)
St Louis, Missouri, U.S.A.

McDonald started performing with Steely Dan in 1974, when he was 18, but left to join The Doobie Brothers the following year. He sang and played on many of their hits such as 'It Keeps You Runnin'' (1976), and 'What a Fool Believes' (1979), which won a Grammy in 1980 for Song of the Year. The Doobie Brothers stopped performing in 1982, and in that same year, he released his first album called *If That's What It Takes*. The most famous song from that album was 'I Keep Forgettin' (Every Time You're Near)', which was sampled in 1994 by Warren G and Nate Dogg on their hit 'Regulate'. Greg Phillanganes played the clavinet on the same song.

McDonald has collaborated with artists such as vocalists Patti LaBelle, Ray Charles, Aretha Franklin and bassist Thundercat. He has won five Grammy Awards and was awarded an honorary degree in 2011 from Berklee College of Music.

'I Can Let Go Now' - If That's What It Takes (1982)

'Our Love' - No Lookin' Back (1985)

'Everlasting' - Blink Of An Eye (1993)

Did you know?
'It Keeps You Runnin'' was featured in the 2004 movie Forrest Gump.

Evelina De Lain performed on a grand piano in the Himalayan Mountains at an altitude of 4,946m! She performed for more than an hour, playing some Chopin and some of her own compositions.

BRIAN MCKNIGHT
(born 1969)
Buffalo, New York, U.S.A.

McKnight began singing at his local church at a young age, inspired by his mother, who played piano in there, and by his older brother, who is part of the legendary vocal group Take 6. McKnight signed his first record deal at 19 and released his first album, *Brian McKnight*, in 1992. That album featured the song 'Never Felt This Way', which was covered by Alicia Keys on her 2003 album Diary Of Alicia Keys. The album *Brian McKnight* also featured one of McKnight's more famous tunes, 'One Last Cry', on which he played keyboards. His 1999 album *Back at One* has sold more than 3 million copies and remains his best-selling album so far.

'Never Felt This Way' - Brian McKnight (1992)

'Anytime' - Anytime (1997)

'Back at One' - Back At One (1999)

McKnight has 17 Grammy nominations but hasn't won any, which ties him with Snoop Dogg. Only Morten Lindberg, with 20, has more non-winning nominations!

A: What do you call a cow that plays the piano?
Q: A Moo-sician!

141

JAMES BOOKER III (1939-83)

Booker performed and recorded with The Doobie Brothers, percussionist Jessie Hill, pianist Fats Domino and drummer Ringo Starr. He released a few records in his lifetime, and a film about him, *Bayou Maharajah: The Tragic Genius of James Booker,* premiered in 2013. Booker once got into trouble with the police, and a district attorney prevented him from going to jail on the condition Booker would give his son piano lessons. That little boy grew up to be multiple-Grammy Award winner Harry Connick Jr!

BOBBY CALDWELL - OPEN YOUR EYES (1980)

This tune was sampled by J Dilla for a song called 'The Light', performed by the rapper Common.

ANITA BAKER - SWEET LOVE (1986)

'Sweet Love' won a Grammy in 1987 for Best R&B Song, and it has been covered or sampled by artists like Beyoncé, MF Doom and Faithless.

ALL MY LIFE - K-CI & JOJO (1997)

This song is from brothers K-Ci and JoJo's first album, *Love Always.* It was nominated for two Grammy Awards, and the video was nominated for best R&B video at the 1998 MTV Video Music Awards.

LUTHER VANDROSS - DANCE WITH MY FATHER (2003)

From the album with the same name, this song won two Grammy Awards in 2004—for Song of the Year and for Best Male R&B Vocal Performance.

GOLDEN - JILL SCOTT (2004)

This song has been featured in a few different films since its release, and it even appears in the video game Grand Theft Auto IV.

The fastest (unofficially) ascending chromatic scale was performed in 6.95 seconds by Hoornaert Nicolas in 2010!

FILM & TV[*]

THE PIANO (1993)

The Piano is about a young woman named Ada (Holly Hunter), who hasn't spoken a word since she was 6, and who expresses herself by playing the piano and relying on her daughter to help interpret. She is sent away to New Zealand by her father in order to get married, but she is separated from her piano and has to earn it back. She falls in love with a man named Baines (Harvey Keitel), and her husband Alisdair (Sam Neill) becomes so angry that he chops off one of her fingers! Ada and Baines leave Alisdair, and Ada learns how to speak again.

---

* Some of these films may not be appropriate for certain age groups.

'Big My Secret' - Michael Nyman

'The Heart Asks Pleasure First' -
Michael Nyman

'The Mood That Passes Through You' -
Michael Nyman

THE PIANIST (2002)

The true story of Władysław Szpilman, a Polish-Jewish pianist, who was well known across Poland and would often play live on the radio. When the Nazis invaded his city of Warsaw, his family were taken to concentration camps, but he managed to escape and survive until the war was over. The movie won three Oscars in 2003 and was ranked number 90 in the BBC's top 100 films of the 21st century. The film soundtrack features many pieces by Chopin.

'Ballade No.1 in G Minor' - Chopin

'Mazurka in A Minor Op. 17, No.4' - Chopin

'Prelude in E Minor, Op. 28, No. 4' - Chopin

Q: What do you call a goat
that plays the piano?
A: Billy Joel!

LA LA LAND (2016)

This movie follows the story of an actress (Emma Stone) and a jazz pianist (Ryan Gosling), who are trying to build their careers. They fall in love and go through many highs and lows before they both achieve their dreams. The movie won six Oscars in 2017 and seven Golden Globe awards.

'Engagement Party' - Justin Hurwitz

'City Of Stars' - Justin Hurwitz

'A Lovely Night' - Justin Hurwitz

GREEN BOOK (2018)

Based on the true story of the African American pianist Don Shirley (Mahershala Ali) and his Italian-American driver/bodyguard Frank Vallelonga (Viggo Mortensen) on Shirley's tour of the American Deep South. *Green Book* is set in the 1960s, which was when many areas of the United States were still segregated. Shirley has to deal with racist attitudes from many people, including Vallelonga, but the two find ways to understand each other and ultimately become friends. It won three Oscars in 2018 and a Golden Globe award for Best Motion Picture.

'Blue Skies' - Kris Bowers

'881 7th Ave' - Kris Bowers

'Dear Dolores' - Kris Bowers

THE SEVENTH VEIL (1945)

The Seventh Veil is a British drama about a pianist named Francesca Cunningham (Ann Todd), who struggles with her mental health and tries to commit suicide. It won an Oscar in 1946 for Best Original Screenplay.

THELONIOUS MONK: STRAIGHT, NO CHASER (1988)

A documentary about jazz pianist Thelonious Monk. It features interviews with his son Thelonious Monk Jr, and behind-the-scenes footage of Monk preparing for recordings, shows and concerts.

RAY (2004)

A dramatic account of 30 years in pianist Ray Charles's life. Charles was played by Jamie Foxx, who won an Oscar, Golden Globe, BAFTA, Critics' Choice and Screen Actors Guild awards for his performance.

'Forrest Gump (Feather Theme)' - Forrest Gump (1994)

'My Heart Will Go On' - Titanic (1997)

'American Beauty Theme' - American Beauty (1999)

'Let It Go' - Frozen (2013)

'Speechless' - Aladdin (2019)

147

MUSICALS

'Funny Honey' - *Chicago* (1975)

'Bugsy Malone' - *Bugsy Malone* (1976)

'Sandy' - *Grease* (1978)

'The Old Gumbie Cat' - *Cats* (1981)

'Seasons of Love' - *Rent* (1994)

'Grandma's Song' - *Billy Elliot* (2000)

'Wig In A Box' - *Hedwig And The Angry Inch* (2001)

'Listen' - *Dreamgirls* (2006)

'What I've Been Looking For' - *High School Musical* (2006)

'The Nicest Kids in Town' - *Hairspray* (2007)

'The Most Beautiful Thing in the World' - *Kinky Boots* (2012)

'Loser Geek Whatever' - *Be More Chill* (2015)

'Waving Through A Window' - *Dear Evan Hansen* (2015)

'The Story of Tonight' - *Hamilton* (2015)

'Omar Sharif' - *The Band's Visit* (2016)

'This is Me' - *The Greatest Showman* (2017)

"Without a piano I don't know how to stand, don't know what to do with my hands." - *Norah Jones*

APPENDIX

CLASSICAL

Domenico Scarlatti (1685–1757)
Christoph Gluck (1714–87)
C.P.E. Bach (1714–88)
Luigi Boccherini (1743–1805)
Antonio Salieri (1750–1825)
Joseph Wölfl (1773–1812)
Nikolaus von Krufft (1779–1818)
Carl Maria von Weber (1786–1826)
Carl Czerny (1791–1857)

English Suite No.5 in E minor - IV. Sarabande - J.S. Bach (c.1713)
Sonata in D minor K.9 - Domenico Scarlatti (1738)
Piano Sonata No.13 in G major - III. Adagio - Haydn (c.1760)
Piano Concerto in C - II. Larghetto - Antonio Salieri (1773)
Violin Sonata in F Major - I. Allegro - Francesca Lebrun (1780)
Piano Concerto No.21 in C major - I. Allegro maestoso - Wolfgang Mozart (1785)
Piano Sonata No.16 in C major - I. Allegro - Wolfgang Mozart (1788)
Piano Concerto No.27 in Bb major - II. Larghetto - Wolfgang Mozart (1791)
Piano Sonata in C minor - I. Adagio - Anton Eberl (1797)
Piano Sonata in B minor - I. Allegro - Joseph Wölfl (1808)

ROMANTIC

Friedrich Burgmüller (1806–74)
Stephen Heller (1813–88)
Wilhelm Kuhe (1823–1912)
Anton Rubinstein (1829–94)
Johannes Brahms (1833–97)
Antonín Dvořák (1841–1904)
Edvard Grieg (1843–1907)
Nikolai Rimsky-Korsakov (1844–1908)
Gabriel Fauré (1845–1924)
Alexander Scriabin (1872–1915)
Mikalojus Čiurlionis (1875–1911)
Robert Nathaniel Dett (1882–1943)

Lieder ohne Worte - Felix Mendelssohn (1829–1845)
Nocturne in C# Minor, B. 49 - Chopin (1830)
Kinderszenen Op. 15 - Robert Schumann (1838)
Lyric Pieces, Book 5, Op. 54 - Edvard Grieg (1867–1901)
24 Preludes Op. 11 - Alexander Scriabin (1888–96)
Sechs Klavierstücke, Op. 118 - Johannes Brahms (1893)
Barcarolle No. 6 In Eb major - Gabriel Fauré (1896)
Vocalise No. 14 - Sergei Rachmaninoff (1912)
In the Bottoms: IV. Barcarolle - Robert Nathaniel Dett (1913)

20TH CENTURY

Erik Satie (1866–1925)
Charles Ives (1874–1954)
Maurice Ravel (1875–1937)
Samuel Coleridge-Taylor (1875–1912)
Artur Schnabel (1882–1951)
Igor Stravinsky (1882–1971)
Rebecca Clarke (1886–1979)
Arthur Rubinstein (1887–1982)
Florence Price (1887–1953)
Myra Hess (1890–1965)
William Grant Still (1895–1978)
Joaquín Rodrigo (1901–99)
Claudio Arrau (1903–91)
Vladimir Horowitz (1903–89)
Olivier Messiaen (1908–92)
Iannis Xenakis (1922–2001)
György Ligeti (1923–2006)
Morton Feldman (1926–87)
Karlheinz Stockhausen (1928–2007)
André Previn (1929–2019)
Alfred Brendel (born 1931)
Glenn Gould (1932–82)
Arvo Pärt (born 1935)
Philip Glass (born 1937)
Daniel Barenboim (born 1942)
Mitsuko Uchida (born 1948)

Gymnopédie No. 1 - Erik Satie (1888)
Je te veux - Erik Satie (1897)
Pavane pour une infante défunte - Maurice Ravel (1899)
Cameos, Op.56: I. Allegro ma non troppo - Samuel Coleridge-Taylor (1904)
Gaspard de la nuit - Maurice Ravel (1908)
Piano Trio II. Andante molto semplice - Maurice Ravel (1921)
Africa I. Land of Peace - William Grant Still (1930)
Romance - Tōru Takemitsu (1949)
Klavierstücke I. Nr. 2 - Karlheinz Stockhausen (1952)
Herma - Iannis Xenakis (1961)
15 Preludes - XIII. Andante cantabile - Nino Rota (1964)
Spiegel im Spiegel - Arvo Pärt (1978)
Études, Book 1: No.1 Désordre - György Ligeti (1985)
For Bunita Marcus - Morton Feldman (1985)
Études, Book 2: No.9 Vertige - György Ligeti (1988 - 94)

Solo Piano - Philip Glass (1989)
Debussy: Preludes - Krystian Zimerman (1993)
Piano Works - John Cage (2013)
Takuya Otaki - Bartók And Virtuosity (2017)
Schoenberg: Piano Music (2019)

21ST CENTURY

Ludovico Einaudi (born 1955)
Hyung-ki Joo (born 1973)
Yui Morishita (born 1981)
Nils Frahm (born 1982)
Vincenzo Maltempo (born 1985)
Olga Scheps (born 1986)
Nobuyuki Tsujii (born 1988)
Isata Kanneh-Mason (born 1996)
Okiem

'Comptine d/Un Autre Été (L'Après-Midi)' - Yann Tiersen (2001)
'River Flows in You' - Yiruma (2001)
'Nuvole Bianche' - Ludovico Einaudi (2004)
'In Time of Silver Rain' - George Walker (2005)
'Ambre' - Nils Frahm (2009)
'Le Onde' - Ludovico Einaudi (2011)
'Space Oddity' - Rick Wakeman (2017)
'New York' - RIOPY (2018)
'Perfect' - The Piano Guys (2018)
'Lion' - J. Cates (2019)
'Opus 31' - Josh McCausland (2019)
'Un piccolo universo' - bzur (2019)

Dragon Songs - Lang Lang (2006)
Syrian Symphony - Malek Jandali (2014)
Kaleidoscope - Khatia Buniatishvili (2016)
Fire On All Sides - James Rhodes (2018)
The Cities - GÅEL (2019)
Florence Price: Piano Discoveries from the Heart - Lara Downes (2020)

RAGTIME

Charles Johnson (1876–1950)
Julius Lenzberg (1878–1956)
Geraldine Dobyns (1882–1956)
Zez Confrey (1895–1971)

'Possum Rag' - Geraldine Dobyns (1907)
'Fig Leaf Rag' - Scott Joplin (1908)
'Crazy Bone Rag' - Charles Johnson (1913)
'Hungarian Rag' - Zez Lenzberg (1913)
'Agitation Rag' - Robert Hampton (1915)
'Jelly Roll Blues' - Jelly Roll Morton (1915)
'The Ragtime Nightingale' - Joseph Lamb (1915)
'Broadway Rag' - James Scott (1922)

The Original James P. Johnson (1973)
Joplin: The Ragtime Dance - Rag and Waltzes - Daniel Blumenthal (1989)
Jelly Roll Morton 1923/24 (1992)

SWING

Lillian Armstrong (1898–1971)
Count Basie (1904–84)
Jesse Stacy (1904–95)
Nat King Cole (1919–65)
Erroll Garner (1921–77)
Dorothy Donegan (1922–98)
Mel Powell (1923–98)
Dave McKenna (1930–2008)

'After You've Gone' - Fats Waller (1930)
'I Wanna Be Happy' - Teddy Wilson (1956)
'That Old Black Magic' - Dorothy Donegan (1957)
'Loose Walk' (Live in Frankfurt) - Count Basie (1988)

Gene Norman Presents an Art Tatum Concert - Art Tatum (1952)
Borderline - Mel Powell Trio (1954)
Concert by the Sea - Erroll Garner (1955)
Solo - Earl Hines (1956)
The Piano Style of Nate King Cole - Nat King Cole (1956)
New Orleans Suite - Duke Ellington (1970)
With Billie in Mind - Teddy Wilson (1972)
My Mama Pinned A Rose On Me - Mary Lou Williams (1978)

BEBOP

Herbie Nichols (1919–63)
Al Haig (1922–82)
Elmo Hope (1923–67)
Red Garland (1923–84)
Joe Albany (1924–88)
Joe Castro (1927–2009)
Phineas Newborn Jr. (1931–89)
Ray Bryant (1931–2011)
Terry Pollard (1931–2009)

'Lady Sings the Blues' - Herbie Nichols Trio (1956)
'Almost Like Being in Love' - Red Garland (1957)
'Isn't It Romantic' - Al Haig Trio (1957)
'Splittin'' - Ray Bryant Trio (1957)
'Stormy Weather' - Oscar Peterson (1959)
'Portrait of Jennie' - Wynton Kelly (1964)
'They Say It's Wonderful' - Joe Albany (1982)

An Evening With Oscar Peterson - Oscar Peterson (1952)
Have You Met Hank Jones (1956)
Brilliant Corners - Thelonious Monk (1957)
Strictly Powell - Bud Powell (1957)
Listen to Barry Harris - Barry Harris (1961)
Here's Hope! - Elmo Hope (1962)
The Great Jazz Piano of Phineas Newborn Jr - Phineas Newborn Jr (1962)
The P.C. Blues - Red Garland (1970)

COOL

Claude Thornhill (1908–65)
Stan Kenton (1911–79)
George Shearing (1919–2011)
John Lewis (1920–2001)
Claude Williamson (1926–2016)
Russ Freeman (1926–2002)
Hampton Hawes (1928–77)
André Previn (1929–2019)

'These Foolish Things' - Lennie Tristano (1956)
'Maria' - André Previn (1959)
'Smoke Gets in Your Eyes' - John Lewis (1959)
'Hip' - Hampton Hawes (1961)
'Over the Rainbow' - George Shearing (1966)

Conversations With Myself - Bill Evans (1963)
Poinciana - Ahmad Jamal (1963)
Time In - Dave Brubeck (1966)
The Awakening - Ahmad Jamal (1970)
Live at Maybeck Recital Hall, Volume Nine - Marion McPartland (1991)

HARD BOP

Gil Evans (1912–88)
Jaki Byard (1922–99)
Jutta Hipp (1925–2003)
Cecil Taylor (1929–2018)
Toshiko Akiyoshi (born 1929)
Horace Parlan (1931–2017)
Sonny Clark (1931–63)
Duke Pearson (1932–80)
Bobby Timmons (1935–74)
Alice Coltrane (1937–2007)
Chucho Valdes (born 1941)
Kenny Barron (born 1943)
Mulgrew Miller (1955–2013)

'Easy Livin'' - Joe Zawinul (1957)
'Two Bass Hit' - Sonny Clark Trio (1957)
'Dat Dere' - Bobby Timmons (1960)
'Long Yellow Road' - Toshiko Akiyoshi (1961)
'Congalegre' - Horace Parlan (1961)
'Scratch' - Kenny Barron (1985)
'Softly As In A Morning Sunrise' - Cedar Walton (1988)
'Solar (Live)' - Kenny Barron Trio (2001)
'It Never Entered My Mind' - Mulgrew Miller and Wingspan (2002)

The Jody Grind - Horace Silver (1967)
Return To Forever - Chick Corea (1972)
Time for Tyner - McCoy Tyner (1973)
Man-Child - Herbie Hancock (1975)
Concerto Retitled - Joe Zawinul (1976)
Piano I - Chucho Valdes (1976)
Trinity - Tommy Flanagan (1980)
Cape Town Revisited - Abdullah Ibrahim (1997)
My Foolish Heart - Keith Jarrett (2007)
A Matter of Black and White (Live at the Keystone Korner - Jaki Byard (2011)
Right On Time - Harold Mabern (2013)
The Art of the Piano Duo (Live) - Kenny Barron & Mulgrew Miller (2019)

CONTEMPORARY

Ray Lema (born 1946)
Jeff Lorber (born 1952)
Sue Keller (born 1952)
Kenny Kirkland (1955–98)
Geri Allen (1957–2017)
Elaine Elias (born 1960)
Bernard Wright (born 1963)
Marcus Roberts (born 1963)
Joey Calderazzo (born 1965)
Jon Medeski (born 1965)
Omar Sosa (born 1965)
Nikki Yeoh (born 1973)
Bill Laurance (born 1981)
Gerald Clayton (born 1984)
Jon Batiste (born 1986)
Cory Henry (born 1987)
Christian Sands (born 1989)

'Chance' - Kenny Kirkland (1991)
'Meeting of the Women' - Paul Hanmer (1997)
'Feed the Fire' - Geri Allen (1997)
'Haiku' - Joey Calderazzo (1999)
'Autumn Leaves' - Michel Petrucciani (2000)
'Ain't Nobody' - Jeff Lorber (2001)
'Human Nature' - Vijay Iyer (2010)
'Ye Bati Koyita' - Samuel Yirga (2011)
'Dusk Baby' - Gerald Clayton (2013)
'His Eye Is On The Sparrow' - John Medeski (2013)
'Sagrado Corazón' - Roberto Fonseca (2016)
'Grüvy' - Connie Han (2018)
'Congo Rhapsody' - Ray Lema (2018)
'Gnawa Sweet' - Joe Armon-Jones (2019)
'My Line' - Reuben James (2020)

Celebration - Bheki Mseleku (1992)
Duke - George Duke (2005)
Quartet - Brad Mehldau (2007)
Double Booked - Robert Glasper (2009)
Place To Be - Hiromi (2010)
Solo Gemini - Nikki Yeoh (2016)
Antiphon - Alfa Mist (2017)
Facing Dragons - Christian Sands (2018)
Beautiful Vinyl Hunter - Ashley Henry (2019)

ROCK

Ray Manzarek (1939–2013)
Jon Lord (1941–2012)
Leon Russell (1942–2016)
Richard Wright (1943–2008)
Tori Amos (born 1963)
Amanda Palmer (born 1976)
Andrew McMahon (born 1982)

'She's a Rainbow' - The Rolling Stones (1967)
'Close to You' - The Carpenters (1970)
'A Song for You' - Leon Russell (1970)
'Song for America' - Kansas (1975)
'The Way It Is' - Bruce Hornsby (1986)
'In Too Deep' - Genesis (1986)
'The End of the Innocence' - Don Henley (1989)
'I Can't Make You Love Me' - Bonnie Raitt (1991)
'El Amor Brujo' - Ray Manzarek (2008)
'Climb' - Tori Amos (2017)

Here's Little Richard - Little Richard (1957)
The Return Of Rock - Jerry Lee Lewis (1965)
Goodbye Yellow Brick Road - Sir Elton John (1973)
52nd Street - Billy Joel (1978)
Absolute Zero - Bruce Hornsby (2019)
Work To Do - Marc Cohn and Blind Boys Of Alabama (2019)

HIP-HOP

'Just a Friend' - Biz Markie (1989) (0:56-1:29)
'Latifah's Had It Up To Here' - Queen Latifah (1991) (1:26-1:45)
'O.P.P.' - Naughty By Nature (1991) (0:09-0:29)
'Regulate' - Warren G ft. Nate Dogg (1994) (0:20-0:40)
'One More Chance/Stay with Me (Remix)' - The Notorious B.I.G ft.
Faith Evans & Mary J. Blige (1995)(0:05-0:46)
'D'evils' - Jay-Z (1996) (0:00-0:11)
'Changes' - 2pac ft. Talent (1998) (0:00-0:13 & 3:53-4:27)
'Thieves in the Night' - Black Star (1998) (0:05-0:47)
'Dance With the Devil' - Immortal Technique (2001) (0:00-0:11)
'Get By' - Talib Kweli (2002) (1:24-1:45)
'Grannie' - J Dilla (2003)
'Go' - Common (2005) (0:00-0:18)
'Been Through The Storm' - Busta Rhymes ft. Stevie Wonder (2006)
(0:32-1:04)
'Everything I Am' - Kanye West ft. DJ Premier (2007) (0:00-0:12)
'Radio Daze' - The Roots (2010) (0:00-0:31)
'Cradle of Civilisation' - Lowkey ft. Mai Khalil (2011)
'Time To Relax' - Akala (2015) (0:00-0:44)
'Trouble' - Kano (2019) (0:04-1:02)

GOSPEL

Ken Medema (born 1943)
Brittani Washington (born 1985)
Alden Clarke
Jason Tyson
Jeremy Jeffers
John Stoddart
Trent Phillips

'People Need The Lord' - Steve Green (1984)
'How Beautiful' - Twila Paris (1990)
'Thank You Lord' - Walter Hawkins (1990)
'The Potter's House' (Live) - Tramaine Hawkins (1990)
'Miracles' - Donald Lawrence and the Tri-City Singers (1993)
'Can't Give Up Now' - Mary Mary (2000)
'He Knows My Name' - Tommy Walker (2000)
'More Than Anything' - Lamar Campbell & Spirit Of Praise (2000) 'We
'Fall Down' - Kyle Matthews (2000)
'I'm Gonna Be Ready' - Yolanda Adams (2001)
'Yes' - Shekinah Glory Ministry (2004)
'Nobody Greater' - VaShawn Mitchell (2010)
'I Know Who I Am' - Sinach (2012)
'Happy' (Live) - Tasha Cobbs Leonard (2013)
'Jesus Is A Love Song' (Live) - The Clark Sisters (2013)
'Exchange' - Brooks and The Company (2015)
'Love Theory' - Kirk Franklin (2019)

Hide 'Em In Your Heart: Bible Memory Melodies (Vol.1) - Steve
Green (1990)
Anthology Live - Richard Smallwood (2015)

POP

Nat Adderley Jr (born 1955)
Jason Freese (born 1972)
Jesse Carmichael (born 1979)
Sara Bareilles (born 1979)
Regina Spektor (born 1980)
Lady Gaga (born 1986)
Brockett Parsons
Hannah Vasanth
Lynette 'Hammondgal' Williams
Oscar Stieler
Michael Patrick
Eugene Roberts

'Think' - Aretha Franklin (1968)
'I Want You Back' - Jackson 5 (1969)
'The Last Time I Saw Richard' - Joni Mitchell (1971)
'Hold The Line' - Toto (1978)
'Wuthering Heights' - Kate Bush (1978)
'How Come U Don't Call Me Anymore?' - Prince (1982)
'Dancing Queen' - ABBA (1986)
'How Am I Supposed To Live Without You' - Michael Bolton (1989)
'Virtual Insanity' - Jamiroquai (1996)
'Beautiful' - Christina Aguilera (2002)
'Bad Day' - Daniel Powter (2005)
'Run' - Leona Lewis (2007)
'Best Thing I Never Had' - Beyoncé (2011)
'A Thousand Years' - Christina Perri (2011)
'When I Was Your Man' - Bruno Mars (2012)

'Read All About It, Pt III' - Emeli Sandé (2012)
'Nina' - Ed Sheeran (2014)
'Stay With Me' - Sam Smith (2014)
'Fool Me Once' - Y'Akoto (2017)
'Zwischen Mann und Kind' - Johannes Oerding (2017)
'Demain c'est toi' - Zaz (2018)
'Cry Today, Smile Tomorrow' - Anthony Ramos (2019)
'Guessing Games' - Buket (2019)
'Guess Who's Back' - Sarajane (2019)
'Kulunako Olwo' - Maurice Kirya (2019)

Songs In A Minor - Alicia Keys (2001)
Once Again - John Legend (2006)

BLUES

Speckled Red (1892–1973)
Leroy Carr (1905–35)
Roosevelt Sykes (1906–83)
Sunnyland Slim (1906–95)
Champion Jack Dupree (1910–92)
Buddy Johnson (1915–77)
Memphis Slim (1915–88)
Jay McShann (1916–2006)
James Booker (1939–83)
Henry Butler (1948–2018)

'44 Blues' - Roosevelt Sykes (1929)
'Honky Tonk Train Blues' - Meade Lux Lewis (1937)
'Heavy Heart Blues' - Champion Jack Dupree (1941)
'Dive Bomber' - Pete Johnson (1944)
'How Long Blues' - Speckled Red (1960)
'Pinetop's Boogie Woogie' - Little Brother Montgomery (1961)
'It Must Have Been the Devil' - Otis Spann (1969)
'You're My Man' - Victoria Spivey (1976)
'Dollar Bill Boogie' - Big Joe Duskin (1978)
'Tanqueray' - Johnnie Johnson (1991)
'Early in the Morning' - Booker T. Laury (1994)

Ray Charles At Newport - Ray Charles (1958)
Gris Gris - Dr. John (1968)
Ladies Man - Pinetop Perkins (2004)

SOUL AND R&B

Renato Neto (born 1965)
Frank McComb (born 1970)
Cassandra O'Neal (born 1973)
PJ Morton (born 1981)

'I Heard It Through The Grapevine' - Marvin Gaye (1968)
'Lean on Me' - Bill Withers (1972)
'Neither One of Us' - Gladys Knight & The Pips (1973)
'Charlene' - Anthony Hamilton (1990)
'Can We Talk' - Tevin Campbell (1993)
'Real Love' - Mary J. Blige (1994)
'Appletree' - Erykah Badu (1997)
'He Loves Me' - Jill Scott (2000)
'I Can Explain' - Rachelle Ferrelle (2000)
'Incomplete' - Sisqo (2000)
'Butterflies' - Michael Jackson (2001)
'Say Yes' - Floetry (2002)
'Window Seat' - Erykah Badu (2010)
'How Deep Is Your Love' - PJ Morton ft. Yebba (2018)

Nina Simone and Piano - Nina Simone (1969)
In Performance - Donny Hathaway (1980)
Natural Wonder - Stevie Wonder (1995)
Soul Speak - Michael McDonald (2008)
An Evening With Brian McKnight - Brian McKnight (2016)
The Piano Album - PJ Morton (2020)

FILM AND TV

Song Without End (1960)
The Chronicle of Anna Magdalena Bach (1968)
Five Easy Pieces (1970)
Lisztomania (1975)
Madame Sousatzka (1988)
Great Balls of Fire! (1989)
Impromptu (1991)
Thirty-Two Short Films About Glenn Gould (1993)
Shine (1996)
The Piano Teacher (2001)
Copying Beethoven (2006)
Four Minutes (2006)
Vitus (2006)
Note by Note: The Making of Steinway L1037 (2007)
Pianomania (2009)
The Piano in a Factory (2010)
Behind the Candelabra (2013)
Grand Piano (2013)
Seymour: An Introduction (2014)
God of the Piano (2019)

'Theme from Schindler's List' (Reprise) - *Schindler's List* (1993)
'Dawn' - *Pride & Prejudice* (2005)
'Bella's Lullaby' - *Twilight* (2008)
'New Moon (The Meadow)' - *Twilight: New Moon* (2009)
'Do You Want to Build a Snowman?' - *Frozen* (2013)
'Mia & Sebastian's Theme' - *La La Land* (2016)

MUSICALS

'One' - *A Chorus Line (1975)*
'Funny Honey' - *Chicago (1975)*
'Bugsy Malone' - *Bugsy Malone (1976)*
'Sandy' - *Grease (1978)*
'Memory' - *Cats (1981)*
'The Old Gumbie Cat' - *Cats (1981)*
'Seasons Of Love' - *Rent (1994)*
'Grandma's Song' - *Billy Elliot (2000)*
'Wig In A Box' - *Hedwig And The Angry Inch (2001)*
'There's a Fine, Fine Line' - *Avenue Q (2003)*
'Listen' - *Dreamgirls (2006)*
'Way Down Hadestown' - *Hadestown (2006)*
'What I've Been Looking For' - *High School Musical (2006)*
'The Nicest Kids in Town' - *Hairspray (2007)*
'The Most Beautiful Thing in the World' - *Kinky Boots (2012)*
'Monster' - *Frozen (2013)*
'Loser Geek Whatever' - *Be More Chill (2015)*
'Waving Through A Window' - *Dear Evan Hansen (2015)*
'The Story of Tonight' - *Hamilton (2015)*
'She Used to Be Mine' - *Waitress (2015)*
'Omar Sharif' - *The Band's Visit (2016)*
'This is Me' - *The Greatest Showman (2017)*

DANCE

'Move Your Body' - Marshall Jefferson (1986)
'Strings of Life' - Derrick May (1987)
'Anthem' - N Joi (1990)
'40 Miles' - Congress (1991)
'Don't Wanna Go' - Sterling Void (1991)
'Northern Piano' - Ultraworld (1991)
'Playing With Knives' - Bizarre Inc (1991)
'Shock The Beat' - Electric Choc (1991)
'I Never Knew Love' - Chez Damier (1992)
'Illusions' - DJ Dove (1994)
'U Sure Do' - Strike (1994)
'Nagasaki' - Ken Doh (1996)
'Needin' U' - David Morales (1998)
'Get Get Down' - Paul Johnson (1999)
'Pjanoo' - Eric Prydz (2008)
'Transformation' - Tim Deluxe (2011)

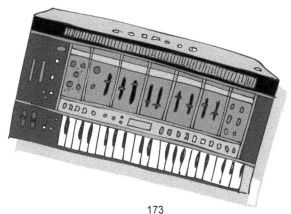

BOOKS

King of Ragtime: Scott Joplin and His Era - Edward A. Berlin (1994)
Piano Lessons: Music, Love, and True Adventures - Noah Adams (1996)
Duke Ellington: A Spiritual Biography (Lives & Legacies) - Janna Tull Steed (1999)
Clara Schumann: The Artist and the Woman - Nancy B. Reich (2001)
The Piano Shop on the Left Bank: The Hidden World of a Paris Atelier – T. E. Carhart (2001)
Bill Evans: How My Heart Sings - Peter Pettinger (2002)
I Put A Spell On You: The Autobiography Of Nina Simone - Nina Simone (2003)
Music for Piano: A Short History - F.E. Kirby (2003)
The Life and Times of Little Richard: The Authorised Biography - Charles White (2003)
Brother Ray: Ray Charles' Own Story - David Ritz and Ray Charles (2004)
Piano Notes: The Hidden World of the Pianist - Charles Rosen (2004)
The Piano - William Miller (2005)
Amadeus - Peter Shaffer (2007)
Blue Monday: Fats Domino and the Lost Dawn of Rock 'n' Roll - Rick Coleman (2007)
Grand Obsession: A Piano Odyssey - Perri Knize (2008)
The Art of French Piano Music: Debussy, Ravel, Fauré, Chabrier - Roy Howat (2009)
The Piano Teacher - Janice Y. K. Lee (2009)
The Story of Boogie-Woogie: A Left Hand Like God - Peter J. Silvester (2009)
Signed, Sealed, and Delivered: The Soulful Journey of Stevie Wonder - Mark Ribowsky (2010)
The Little Piano Girl: The Story of Mary Lou Williams, Jazz Legend - Ann Ingalls & Maryann Macdonald (2010)
Thelonious Monk: The Life and Times of an American Original - Robin D. G. Kelley (2010)

A Natural History of the Piano: The Instrument, the Music, the Musicians—from Mozart to Modern Jazz and Everything in Between - Stuart Isacoff (2011)

Mozart and His Piano Concertos - Cuthbert Girdlestone (2011)

Shall We Play That One Together? Paul de Barros (2012)

Anita's Piano: A Witness to History - Marion Stahl and Anita Ron Schorr (2014)

Herbie Hancock: Possibilities - Herbie Hancock, with Lisa Dickey (2014)

Billy Joel - Fred Schruers (2015)

Piano Man: Life of John Ogdon - Charles Beauclerk (2015)

Franz Liszt: Musician, Celebrity, Superstar - Oliver Hilmes (2016)

The Music of Life: Bartolomeo Cristofori & the Invention of the Piano - Elizabeth Rusch (2017)

Me: Elton John (Official Autobiography) - Elton John (2019)

Piano Lessons: Reflection from a LIFE in Music - Vladimir Feltsman (2019)

Total Praise: The Autobiography of Richard Smallwood - Richard Smallwood (2019)

Hitler's Piano Player: The Rise and Fall of Ernst Hanfstaengl, Confidant of Hitler, Ally of Roosevelt - Peter Conradi (2020)

More Myself: A Journey - Alicia Keys (2020)

Soul on Soul: The Life of Mary Lou Williams - Tammy L. Kernodle (2020)

The Lost Pianos of Siberia - Sophy Roberts (2020)

ANSWERS

Q1: b) Storm and Stress
Q2: a) 11
Q3: d) a starling
Q4: a) Für Elise
Q5: a) The Simpsons AND b) Phineas and Ferb
Q6: c) 31,073
Q7: d) Zen Buddhism
Q8: a) Thelonious Monk
Q9: c) Mary Lou Williams
Q10: d) Red Garland
Q11: d) The Sopranos
Q12: d) Michael Jackson
Q13: c) Jerry Lee Lewis
Q14: a) 7

ACKNOWLEDGEMENTS

I have to give a huge thank you to my amazing consultants Rachel Murphy, Josiah Williams, Khalia Williams, Josiah Francis, Aydon Oyedele and Jaheim Roman—never let anybody limit you.

The lady responsible for all of these amazing illustrations, Charity Russell. Without your touch, this book would just be another mini-encyclopaedia. Your drawings brought all these fabulous musicians and facts to life. Thank you.

My amazing editor, Joel Drazner. You took my muddled words, shaped them, and provided a sense of order that I never could have done by myself. Seriously, there would be zero commas in this book if it were up to me. A true professional and a gentleman. Thank you.

Paul Vernon! We met in such an unconventional way, but you gave me that extra push to press on and get this book done. Your support, feedback and help were, and continue to be, invaluable.

A special thank you to Becca Toft, Rachel Francis, Daniel Holder, Akil Henry, Ben Burrell, Sarah Aluko, Amy Hurford, Renato Paris, Natalie Latus, Tony Turrell, Scholar, Simon Lee, Lorraine Liyange, Shomari Williams, Melissa Ogbonna, Varo Sisti, Sabine Zengerling, Christina Fontaine, Aisha Charles, Conrad Benjamin and Michaela Mathieu-Marius for the messages, proofreading, support and love.

INDEX

ABOUT THE AUTHOR

Nathan Holder is a musician, author and consultant based in London. He received his Masters in Music Performance from Kingston University, while winning the MMus Prize for Outstanding Achievement. As a musician, he has performed with artists such as Ed Sheeran, The Arkells and Zoe Birkett, and performed in locations in Dubai, Bali, USA and across Europe. His first book published in 2018 is called I Wish I Didn't Quit: Music Lessons.

CPSIA information can be obtained
at www.ICGtesting.com
Printed in the USA
LVHW051314280820
664255LV00007B/455